# FILM POSTERS
## EXPLOITATION

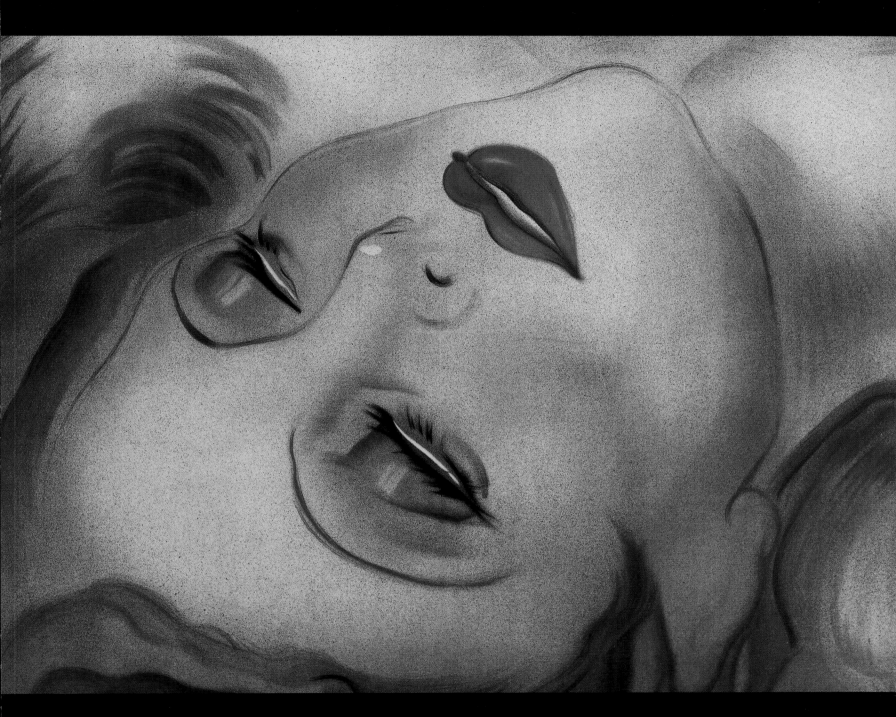

# FILM POSTERS
## EXPLOITATION

**edited by tony nourmand and graham marsh**
**foreword by dave kehr**

EVERGREEN

EVERGREEN is an imprint of
TASCHEN GmbH

© 2006 TASCHEN GmbH
Hohenzollernring 53, D-50672 Köln
**www.taschen.com**

ISBN 978-3-8228-5625-3

Printed in Singapore

Art direction and design by Graham Marsh
Text by Tony Nourmand and Alison Aitchison
Research and co-ordination by Alison Aitchison
Page layout by Trevor Gray
Text edited by Roxanna Hajiani
Proof-reading by Roxanna Hajiani and Alison Aitchison
Principal conservation by Eric Jean-Baptiste
Principal photography by A.J. Photographics

Unless otherwise stated, all images used in this book
are from The Reel Poster Archive

**ACKNOWLEDGEMENTS**

Tarek AbuZayyad
Richard & Barbara Allen
Farhad Amirahmadi
Martin Bridgewater
Kamyar Broumand
Otto Buj
Joe Burtis
Mr & Mrs P. Cakes
Glyn Callingham
Andrew Cohen
Emma Copley
Tony Crawley
Chris Dark
Fabyan Daw
Greg Ferland
Leslie Gardner
The Haldane Collection
Helmut Hamm
The Hastings Collection
Sarah Hodgson
Roberto Hoornweg
Yoshikazu Inoue
Eric & Prim Jean-Baptiste
Andy Johnson
Wayne Joseph
John & Billie Kisch
Peter & Betty Langs
Richard Loncraine
Andrew MacDonald
Krzysztof Marcinkiewicz
June Marsh
Philip Masheter
Kirby McDaniel
Tomoaki 'Nigo' Nagao
Hamid and Doris Nourmand
The Nouvelle Vague Collection
Separate Cinema
Philip Shalam
Mo Sheikh-Kadir
Dan Strebin
Simon Tapson
Liza Tesei
The Crew From The Island
The X-Rated Collection
and Kim Goddard

Special thanks to Bruce Marchant; without his help,
these books would not be possible.

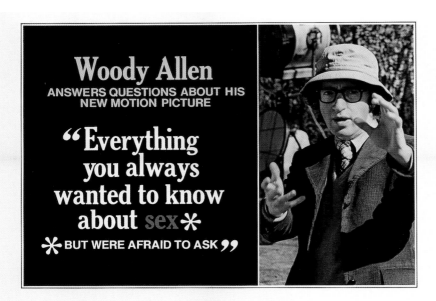

**Everything You Always Wanted To Know About Sex …** (1972)
US 41 × 27 in. (104 × 69 cm)
(Advance)
Courtesy of the Tony Nourmand Collection

# CONTENTS

# FOREWORD

Tony Nourmand and Graham Marsh have focused previous books in their series on film poster art on well-defined, discrete genres: the science-fiction film, horror movies, the thriller as practiced by Alfred Hitchcock.

The exploitation film is something else. Whereas classical genres like the western or the detective film depend on a base collection of stock characters, themes and situations, exploitation films can, and do, draw on a range of subjects as wide as fiction itself, from the innocent burlesque of the late 50s 'nudies' like Russ Meyer's *The Immoral Mr. Teas* to the ketchup-soaked sadism of a 60s shocker like Herschell Gordon Lewis's *Color Me Blood Red*. An exploitation film can be about childbirth or venereal disease, drug abuse or drag racing, a dance craze or crime spree. It may be the one genre defined not by content, but by attitude – a certain willingness on the part of filmmakers, and an unbridled enthusiasm on the part of exhibitors, to appeal to the public's less noble impulses.

It's not a secret that sex sells. It has been selling ever since Thomas A. Edison successfully commercialized motion picture entertainment in the 1890s, with two-minute cheesecake films like *Fatima, Muscle Dancer* and *Annabelle Serpentine Dance* (both 1895). Violence, the second horseman of the exploitation apocalypse, appears with relish in Edison's *The Execution Of Mary, Queen Of Scots* (another 1895 release) and reaches a truly bizarre extreme in the 1903 *Electrocuting An Elephant* (which, unlike so many exploitation films, delivers precisely what it promises – the spectacle of a rogue elephant being electrocuted at Coney Island).

But wherever sex and violence can be found, censors will surely follow. It took very little time for civic groups to begin cracking down on the new medium, denouncing the nickelodeons as dens of vice that encouraged drinking, prostitution and lack of respect toward one's betters (it was not a coincidence that the censors came from the patrician class, while much of the audience for early film consisted of working-class immigrants).

The censors and the filmmakers shared one thing: a love of publicity. Soon, the two sides discovered that their's could be a mutually beneficial relationship. The clergymen and politicians could make headlines and please their constituents by loudly denouncing the immorality of the new medium; the filmmakers and exhibitors were more than grateful for the unpaid advertising that drew public attention to their wares. When the authorities declined to be drawn, later generations of exploitation filmmakers sent advance men into communities to stir up controversy where none existed. One favourite tactic was to hire pickets to march up and down in front of the theatres that 'dared' to show these 'startling exposés', a spectacle always guaranteed to attract attention and stimulate ticket sales.

In a sense, it's the dance between the censor and the filmmaker that defines the exploitation film. Without the censor to set limits, the exploitation filmmaker has nothing to defy. Or rather, pretend to defy, since few if any exploitation filmmakers had a commitment to their art that stretched to going to jail. Plainly pornographic material,

which had also existed since the birth of cinema, was born underground and lived underground, shown in Parisian brothels or fraternity smokers. But exploitation thrives on the margins of legality, promising to show the unshowable but never, in reality, quite crossing the line.

In Ted Bonnitt's enjoyable documentary on the exploitation business, *Mau Mau Sex Sex* (2001), the veteran exploitation producer David Friedman defines the appeal of the genre in terms of audience expectations: 'Well, we didn't see it this week – but next week, we'll see it for sure!' Friedman, who worked in every exploitation sub-genre from nudist camp movies (*Nature's Playmates*, 1962) to Nazi porn (*Ilsa, She Wolf Of The SS*, 1975), left the business after pornography emerged into the (semi) mainstream in the late 70s. Once everything could be shown, there was no more tease, no more creative dodging of the limits and, for Friedman, no more fun. Today, at the age of 81, Friedman operates a small carnival in the southern United States, a return to the quaint, one-on-one hucksterism that drew him to the business in the first place.

One of the earliest tactics filmmakers used to evade the censors was to play the latter's own game, by pretending to denounce various social evils – drug abuse, the white slave traffic – that they would then go on to depict in loving detail. George Loane Tucker's 1913 *Traffic In Souls*, among the first American feature-length films, employed this technique with its tale of a plucky young woman searching for her sister, who has been kidnapped by a white slave ring (the head of the ring is revealed to be a millionaire philanthropist, in a climax that must have particularly pleased the immigrant audience). Mrs Wallace Reid, the widow of the silent film star who died of alcohol and morphine addiction, produced and starred in *Human Wreckage* (1923), the story of a crusading attorney's battle with drug dealers (and launched her own career, as one of Hollywood's handful of female writers and directors, as a result).

White slavery remained a central theme through the 30s and 40s, as illustrated by several posters in this book. The 1937 *Slaves In Bondage* promised 'uncensored secrets of the Nations [sic] sinister vice scandals', along with visions of 'girls ensnared into lives of shame!'. *The Vice Racket* (1936, also known as *Gambling With Souls*), promised to 'blast the truth before your eyes', about 'scarlet girls chained to the vultures of vice'. *Main Street Girls* (1936) offered 'a thundering indictment of crooked prison parole boards' while *Secrets Of A Model* promised to 'bare the private lives of the glamorous girls in glittering Hollywood'.

Following in Mrs Reid's footsteps, anti-drug films proliferated as well. *Assassin Of Youth* (1937), *The Devil's Harvest* (1942) and *Tell Your Children* (1938, better known under its many re-release titles, including *The Burning Question* and *Reefer Madness*) all unflinchingly investigated the curse of marijuana, with a particular emphasis on one of the drug's lesser known side-effects – its tendency to lead innocent young women to strip down to their lacy

**Youth Aflame** (1944)
US 41 × 27 in. (104 × 69 cm)
Courtesy of the Tony Nourmand Collection

underthings. (One interesting footnote to this genre is the case of *Big Jim McLain*, a John Wayne adventure in which he played a swashbuckling investigator for the anti-Communist House Un-American Activities Committee. Because audiences outside the US didn't know or care about HUAC, new dialogue was written for the French and Italian dubbed versions that turned Wayne's character into a drug investigator, and the film was released in those territories as *Marijuana*.)

The 30s brought a whole new raft of social evils for the crusading filmmakers to denounce, including abortion (*Sinful Souls*, 1939), venereal disease (*Damaged Goods*, 1937), and the seemingly wide-spread menace of gorillas having sex with young white women ('Wild Women! Wild Beasts!' promised the 1934 *Forbidden Adventure*). But the 30s brought an even greater gift when Hollywood began vigorously enforcing the Production Code in 1934, effectively putting the studios (Paramount, in particular) out of the titillation business.

Whereas a film like *Sign Of The Cross* (1932) could briefly depict bare breasts, enthusiastic whipping, and intimations of homo-sexuality, those options were no longer available to the studios once the Code came into effect. As a result, many of the subjects prohibited by the Code – they included adultery, 'lustful' kissing, 'seduction or rape' (apparently interchangeable notions), 'sex perver-sion', white slavery, miscegenation, sex hygiene and scenes of childbirth – fell directly into the laps of the exploitationers, who were not signatories to the Code. All an exploitation producer in search of a topic had to do was to read the list of 'repellent subjects' banned by the Code – and there was his script.

Exhibitors who didn't want to go to the trouble of producing their own exploitation films for the US market could simply turn to Europe, where filmmaking remained relatively unimpeded by censorship. Made in 1933, Gustav Machaty's Czech film *Ecstasy* did not make it to the United States until 1940, by which time its leading actress, billed as 'Hedy Kiesler', had become Hedy Lamarr, Hollywood star. 'Art-house' theatres opened in major cities in the US and UK to showcase continental imports, which offered 'adult' subjects, such as flashes of nudity that could not be seen in the domestic product.

Subtitles served to remind patrons (and censors) that what they were seeing was a high-cultural product, uncontaminated by base, exploitative motives. The alibi worked so well that even a hardened exploitation distributor like Kroger Babb (whose *Mom And Dad*, a childbirth film, was one of the genre's biggest hits) could buy an Ingmar Bergman film, *Summer With Monica*, retitle it *Monica, The Story Of A Bad Girl* and drop it into art-house distribution, to the satisfaction of both cinephiles and passing voyeurs. Roger Vadim's *... And God Created Woman* (1956) proved to be the tipping point in

this particular dodge. With its frank sexuality and copious nudity on the part of Vadim's young discovery, Brigitte Bardot, the film became an international hit, helping to create a distribution model for foreign films that greatly benefited the French New Wave directors when they emerged three years later.

'Art films' like *... And God Created Woman* opened the way for American-made nudies, such as David Freidman's francophilic *The Adventures Of Lucky Pierre* (1961) or Doris Wishman's poetically bizarre *Nude On The Moon* (1962). These films, which included many of Russ Meyer's early efforts, were essentially animated versions of the pin-ups appearing in the men's magazines of the period, particularly *Playboy*, and were all about looking rather than touching – they contained even less sexual activity than the average Hollywood film. This strange state of affairs continued through the 60s, contributing to a massive sense of stimulation without release that led to the phenomenon of the 'roughies' – films like Wishman's *Bad Girls Go To Hell* (1965) or Lee Frost's *The Defilers* (1965), in which sexual frustration was channelled into physical abuse.

The beginning of the end for the exploitation industry came with Vilgot Sjoman's Swedish film *I Am Curious (Yellow)*, a 1967 import that survived several court battles in the US to become a tremendous moneymaker for its distributor, Grove Press. Employing the ancient 'redeeming social value' dodge, the film managed to smuggle a glimpse of oral sex into American theatres, and so opened the floodgates that admitted Gerard Damiano's *Deep Throat* in 1972 and the wave of hardcore pornographic films that followed. Now that nothing was forbidden, there was nothing to exploit – the audience's expectations, once so artfully teased, could now be bluntly and banally fulfilled.

Today, the exploitation aesthetic survives mainly as camp – self-conscious evocations of the old outrageousness, sometimes clever (as in the early work of John Waters and the films of George Kuchar), sometimes merely crude (as in the hundreds of direct-to-video films released each year, with titles like *Sorority Babes In The Slimeball Bowl-O-Rama* or *Hollywood Chainsaw Hookers*).

The old outrageousness, however, is still very much with us, in the form of the astonishing advertising material issued by the exploitation distributors. Many of the posters lovingly reproduced in this book seem to represent much more care and effort on the part of their creators than went into the films they promote. And that, perhaps, is how it should be, in an industry whose motto has always been 'sell the sizzle, not the steak'. There is much to enjoy in the shocking, scandalous, frank, bold and daring pages that follow.

**Dave Kehr**
April 2005

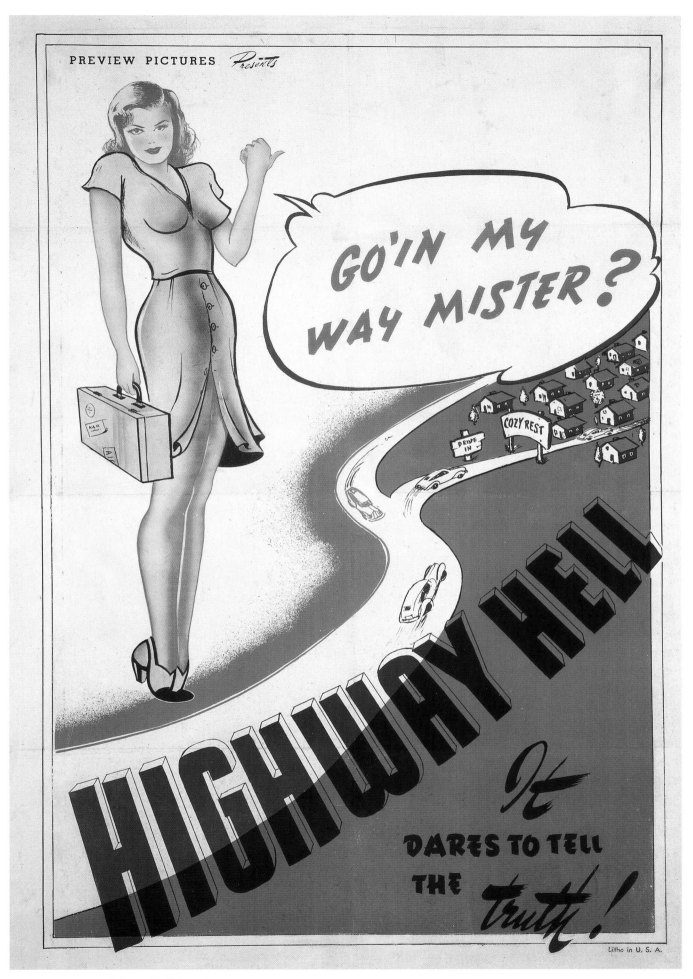

**Hitchhike To Hell (Highway Hell)** (1937)
US 41 × 27 in. (104 × 69 cm)

# MISSING FROM THE MAINSTREAM

Films and their associated poster art always provide us with an interesting window into the past and this is particularly true of the exploitation genre – few things tell us as much about the lives of earlier generations as their secret fears and taboos. When we were sifting through options for this book, we were struck by just how much times have changed. Describing marijuana as the 'smoke of hell' or teenagers as 'heedless youth speeding through life with the throttle wide open' sounds ridiculously over the top to us today but these were words that obviously reflected real and widespread concerns half a century ago. And sometimes the changes in social attitudes can take place in a remarkably short time. The title of the Austin Powers movie, *The Spy Who Shagged Me*, scarcely raised an eyebrow when it was released in 1999, but as recently as 1990 the original poster for *Dick Tracy*, a tame Disney flick, was banned for its overtly suggestive tagline, 'Mind if I call you Dick?' Yet, while some things change, others do not, and the exploitation of women has remained a depressingly consistent feature of the genre from its inception right up to the present. However much times have changed in other respects, sex is still used to sell as many films today as it did in the 20s.

Of all film genres, exploitation is possibly the one that lends itself best to the use of posters as a promotional medium. Screaming taglines, provocative titles and scantily-clad women are all elements that can be used to best advantage in poster form. So much so that, as our research progressed, we came to see that the real criterion for including a poster in this book was not so much that it had been created to promote an exploitation film, but rather the exploitative nature of the poster itself. Thus the book is indeed devoted to exploitation *poster art*.

Posters for titles like *Flesh And The Devil* and *Tarzan And His Mate* (both by noted artist William Galbraith Crawford) feature artwork that exploits the sexy and alluring elements of the films. The films themselves are not classic 'exploitation', though, like many pre-Hays Code Hollywood films, they include surprisingly risqué scenes (but the censors did remove a bold, naked underwater sequence that originally featured in *Tarzan And His Mate*). The fact that these were movies produced by big mainline studios does not make the posters any less exploitative. However, many of the titles featured in this book did originate in the traditional, independent exploitation industry and in these cases it is only the posters that have endured. Films like *The Acid Eaters* and *Youth Aflame* were classic, low-budget exploitation affairs that have been forgotten as films, but are remembered for their fantastic exploitation poster art. Because of the nature of the Hollywood studio system and the number of independent filmmakers working in the exploitation genre, many of the posters featured in this book are by uncredited artists; however, this does not detract from their impact. The anonymous artwork for *Way Out* for example, is simple yet remains hauntingly striking.

This said, the book does also feature work by a number of renowned artists and designers. McClelland Barclay is most famous for his depictions of beautiful women and his poster for *Hotel For Women* illustrates this aspect of his art perfectly. He was working in the 30s, at the same time as two other influential poster designers, Alberto Vargas and 'Hap' Hadley. Vargas was famous for his glamorous portraits of pin-up stars and paintings of the female nude and this skill is reflected in the artwork for *The Sin Of Nora Moran* and *Ladies They Talk About*. Hadley is recognized as one of the most adventurous and influential caricaturists of his era and his artwork for *Cock Of The Air* epitomises his quirky style.

Two of the most striking posters in *Exploitation Poster Art* are those produced for *Extase* and *Mädchen In Uniform* by Carlo Mariani, a French artist working in the 30s whose work was heavily influenced by the Art Deco movement. It was another French artist, Roger Rojac, working mainly in the 40s and 50s, who was responsible for the poster for *La Putain Respectueuse*.

The posters featured in this book cover a vast range, from the cheap, sensationalist products of the exploitation roadshow men to the slick, professional output of Hollywood publicists. Their styles also vary enormously both from film to film, and from country to country. Similarly, the artists whose work is featured are from diverse backgrounds: they include regular studio artists, famous graphic designers, glamour photographers and comic-book illustrators. The last category includes Robert Crumb, one of the most renowned and influential comic-book artists of the twentieth century, whose poster art for *Fritz The Cat* depicts one of his most famous creations.

In the 60s and 70s, in a change that reflected the more liberal attitudes of the period, established and respected artists became involved in the campaigns for films that an earlier generation would have considered beyond the pale. The renowned designer Steve Frankfurt, for example, was hired to work on the American poster campaign for the soft-porn masterpiece *Emmanuelle* and his willingness to become involved is a testament to the credibility that the new 'porno chic' movement had achieved at that point. Similarly, Alan Aldridge, a famous and important graphic designer of the 60s, was responsible for the poster for Andy Warhol's avant-garde *Chelsea Girls*, which remains one of his most famous works.

The majority of the posters featured in this book will be entirely new to its readers. This is partly due to the fact that exploitation has never received the same attention as more traditional genres like science fiction or film noir. Another factor is that independent, exploitation filmmakers worked with extremely low budgets and many of the posters for their films were printed on cheap stock with small print-runs, with the result that fewer have actually survived. In making our selection for this book, we have tried to provide a flavour of all the many facets of this fascinating genre and we now invite you to relax and feel your 'senses drowned in forbidden pleasures!' One word of caution, though: 'Beware the cost of a little fun!'

**Tony Nourmand** and **Graham Marsh**
May 2005

# POOR WHITE TRASH

## See How They Live

**Bayou (Poor White Trash)** (1957)
US 41 × 27 in. (104 × 69 cm)
Courtesy of the Haldane Collection

**Traffic In Souls** (1913)
US 41 × 27 in. (104 × 69 cm)

In 1913 the Rockefeller Commission released a report claiming that police corruption was to blame for the proliferation of prostitution and the white slave trade. Among the victims were female immigrants to the US, many travelling alone, whose vulnerability was only increased when the people who were supposed to offer protection sought to profit from their plight. While the press enjoyed a field day, turning the report into the year's biggest story, Universal Studios also capitalized on the situation by releasing *Traffic In Souls*. At the time, the film was one of the most expensive and sophisticated features ever made. It cost $25,000 to produce and a separate unit was established to handle an advertising campaign with a budget of $1000 a week. Approved by the New York censors, *Traffic In Souls* was a massive success, playing to audiences totalling over 30,000 during its opening week on Broadway.

Within a few months, a second film, *The Inside Of The White Slave Traffic*, took up the same theme. Its producers pioneered many of the publicity techniques that would later be adopted by the exploitation industry in the 20s and 30s. The film was promoted as being based on fact and the posters made much of the point that its writer and director, Samuel H. London, was the former head of staff of the Rockefeller Commission. In an attempt to emphasize the redeeming moral qualities of his picture, London named his production company 'The Moral Feature Film Company'. Despite this, the censors were not convinced of the purity of the producers' motives and judged that the film would have a corrupting influence on young men. The trade paper *Variety* warned that it lowered the tone of the whole industry. Despite, or perhaps because of this, it was a hit with audiences.

**The Inside Of The White Slave Traffic** (1913)
US 41 × 27 in. (104 × 69 cm)

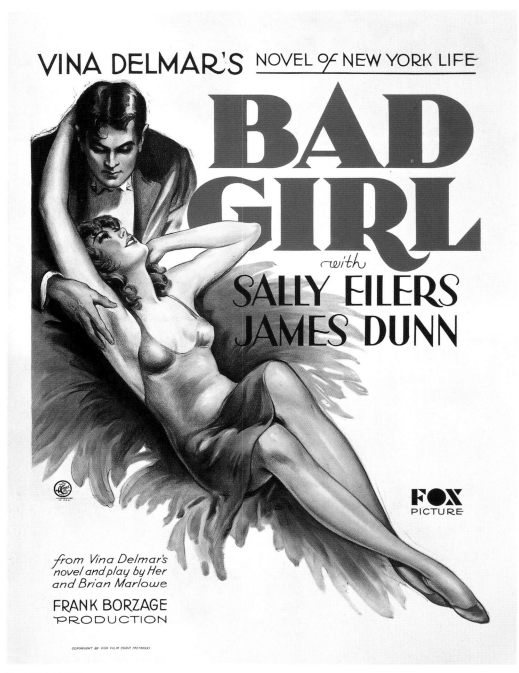

**Bad Girl** (1931)
US 41 × 27 in. (104 × 69 cm)
(Style B)

In pre-20s Hollywood, little effort was made to impose restrictions upon either the content of films or the ways in which they were advertised. Although censorship existed, it had very little influence when set against the power of the major studios. Later, during the 20s and early 30s, the industry came under increasing pressure from both the churches and political leaders who were eager to rein in a Hollywood which they considered to be setting the country an appalling example with its debauchery and moral bankruptcy. Their arguments gained both strength and publicity as a result of a number of notorious Hollywood scandals. Two of the most shocking concerned the death of Wallace Reid from influenza, brought on by drug-abuse, and Fatty Arbuckle's arrest for the alleged rape and murder of a young actress who had been a participant in an all-night alcohol- and drug-fuelled 'orgy' he was hosting (he was later cleared of all charges). The critics were further provoked by Hollywood's continuing preference for giving its films titles like *Bad Girl* and *The Brat*, and its use of equally suggestive posters to promote them.

● **1896.** *The Irwin Rice Kiss* is the first film criticized for its content, which included a close-up of a prolonged kiss.
● **1906.** The mayor of New York closes all cinemas on the grounds of 'safety' and refuses to show any films of dubious moral value.
● **1907.** The first motion picture censorship law is passed in Chicago, where a police permit is required before any film can be shown to the public.
● **1911.** Pennsylvania is the first state to establish a censorship board.
● **1921.** The 'Thirteen Points' are introduced in Hollywood in an attempt to provide a moral framework for the film industry.
● **1927.** The 'Don'ts And Be Carefuls' set of moral guidelines are introduced in Hollywood as a precursor to the Hays Code.
● **1929.** Over 2500 cities have adopted some form of censorship law.
● **1930.** The Hays Code is introduced.
● **1934.** The Hays Code is strictly enforced.

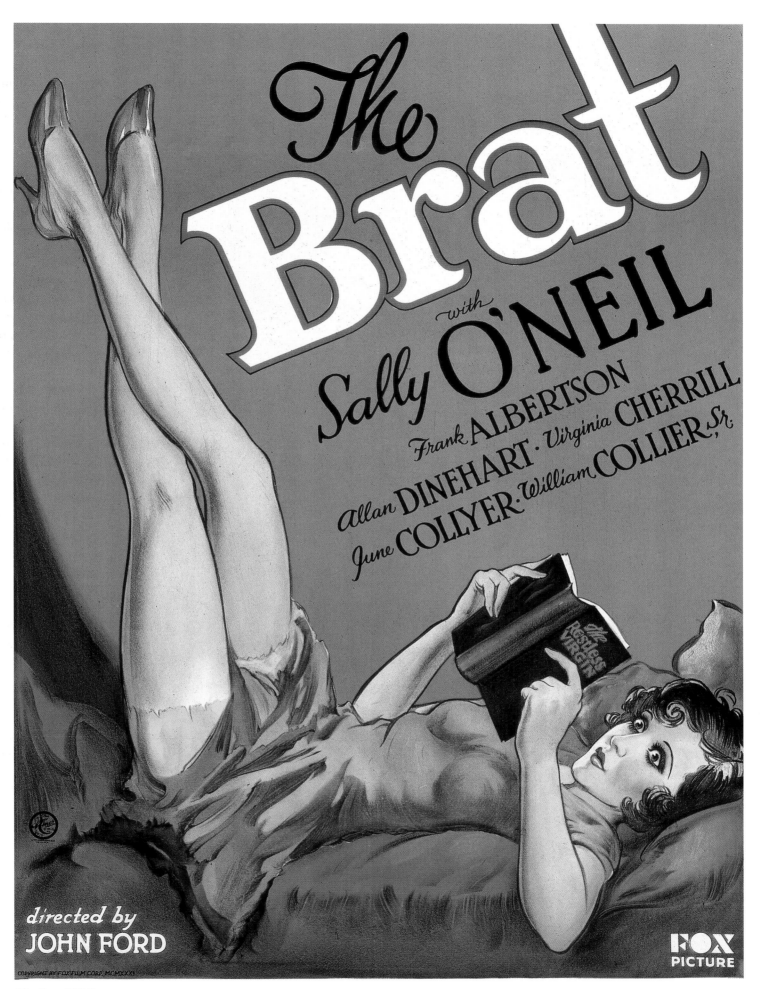

**The Brat** (1931)
US 41 × 27 in. (104 × 69 cm)

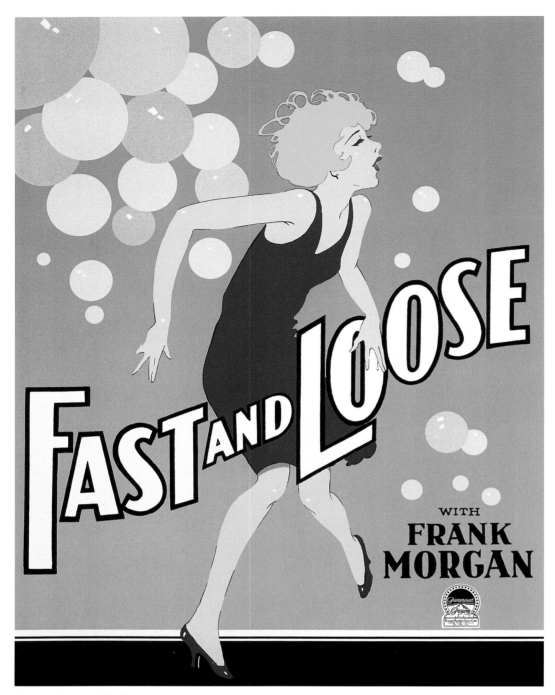

**Fast And Loose** (1930)
US 22 × 14 in. (56 × 36 cm)

The Hollywood establishment made its first attempt at self-restraint at the beginning of the 20s, when **William H. Hays** (1879–1954) was hired as president of the Motion Picture Producers and Distributors of America. He introduced, successively, 'Thirteen Points Of Standard' (1921), The 'Don'ts And Be Carefuls' (1927) and the 'Production Code' (1930). Although these rules did have some limited effect, they were largely ignored or bypassed by the studios. Moreover, since the promotional activities of the industry were not subject to any form of code or scrutiny, it was always possible to make up for any lack of explicit content in the films themselves by using poster imagery that was often extremely suggestive; similarly, film titles and taglines loaded with sexual innuendo were regularly used to attract audiences to movies that often promised a good deal more than they actually delivered.

Ultimately, it was the placing of a particularly provocative billboard poster outside a church that brought matters to a head. The complaints of the priest concerned encouraged the formation of a pressure group, The Catholic Legion of Decency, which boycotted the industry until it cleaned up its act. Belatedly recognizing that the pressure for censorship was becoming irresistible, Hollywood bowed to the inevitable and agreed to abide by the rules of the new Hays Code, which became mandatory rather than simply advisory and was applied not only to the content of films but also to the advertising material used to promote them. Joseph L. Breen was hired as director of the Production Code Administration which had to give every film a seal of approval before it could be released. Almost overnight, Hollywood abandoned its carefree, anything-goes attitude and was forced to accept a system in which its products were subjected to censorship of the most rigorous and nit-picking kind.

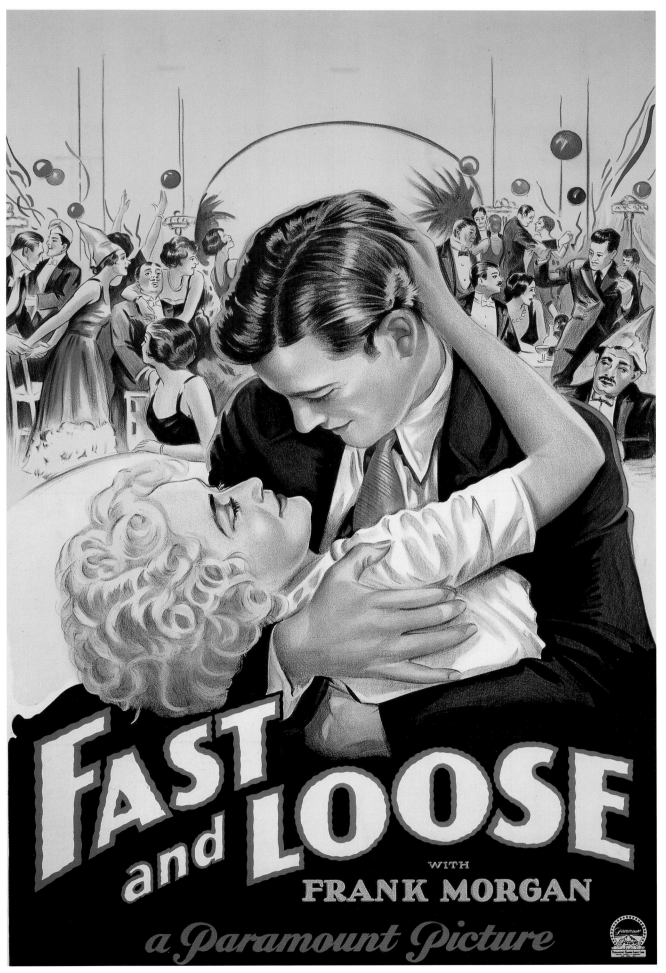

**Fast And Loose** (1930)
US 41 × 27 in. (104 × 69 cm)

**Uncivilized** (1936)
US 22 × 14 in. (56 × 36 cm)
Courtesy of the Tony Nourmand Collection

The Hays Code was long and detailed and it covered every aspect of filmmaking, from camera angles to plot lines. Amongst much else, it stipulated that:

● 'No picture shall be produced which will lower the moral standards of those who see it.'
● 'The illegal drug traffic must not be portrayed … nor shall such scenes be approved which show the use of illegal drugs, or their effects, in detail.'
● 'The use of liquor in American life … will not be shown.'
● 'Adultery and illicit sex … must not be explicitly treated or justified, or presented attractively.'
● 'Excessive and lustful kissing, lustful embraces, suggestive postures and gestures are not to be shown.'
● 'Sex perversion or any inference to it is forbidden.'
● 'White slavery shall not be treated.'
● 'Sex relationships between the white and black races are forbidden.'
● 'Sex hygiene and venereal disease are not proper subjects for theatrical motion pictures.'
● 'Scenes of actual childbirth … are never to be presented.'
● 'Abortion shall never be shown explicitly or by inference, and … [the] word 'abortion' shall never be used.'
● 'Complete nudity is never permitted.'
● 'Undressing scenes should be avoided … and indecent or undue exposure is forbidden.'
● 'Dances which emphasize indecent movements are to be regarded as obscene.'
● 'Salacious, indecent, or obscene titles shall not be used.'

The burgeoning exploitation industry took these guidelines and used them as a blueprint to specify exactly what its audiences wanted. Over the 34 years that the Hays Code remained in place, the exploitation filmmakers would take these rules and break each and every one of them.

**A Fig Leaf For Eve** (1944)
US 41 × 27 in. (104 × 69 cm)
Courtesy of the Tony Nourmand Collection

**The Seventh Commandment** (1933)
US 41 × 27 in. (104 × 69 cm)
Courtesy of the Tony Nourmand Collection

The exploitation industry had existed from the early 20s, but it flourished under the Hays Code. Before 50s 'B' movies, 60s sexploitation and 70s blaxploitation, exploitation was a very different, and much cruder affair. Indeed, the 'industry' was little more than a small group of savvy businessmen who became independent filmmakers and travelled the country pedalling their products. They became known as the 'Forty Thieves' and had more in common with the carnival and circus tradition than with the mainline movie business. Their films were cheaply made, badly acted and of a generally poor standard, yet they offered audiences something Hollywood couldn't: titillation. They took every subject that was forbidden or considered taboo and exploited its earning capacity to the limit.

The roadshow men did everything themselves, from writing and directing their films to distributing and promoting them. They would sometimes try to get approval from the Breen Office by screening a heavily censored print of their product, but more often than not they would take the uncensored version on the road with them, travelling from state to state. They would then either come to an arrangement by which the local theatre owner agreed to screen the film, or, if this didn't work, they would set up a tent on the edge of town, with a sheet for a screen and wooden benches as seats. They would then start the task of drumming up an audience and this is how the industry acquired its title of 'exploitation'.

Their poster art was not distinguished for its subtlety. Posters headed with provocative titles promised 'Startling Revelations!' and 'Shocking Truths!' against a backdrop of female flesh. But they did not limit their promotional activities to bill-posting and much of it was aimed at reassuring their audiences that, rather than simply watching a 'dirty film', they were participating in a worthy social cause. Thus, 'educational' pamphlets and books were sold to audiences watching films on venereal disease, vice films featured a voice-over proclaiming the moral necessity of teaching the young the facts of life and, for one drug film, the corpse of a victim of drug-abuse was rigged up in a cage outside the theatre. Any and every gimmick that could bolster sales and profits was used.

Dwain Esper is perhaps the most famous of the Forty Thieves and *The Seventh Commandment* was his earliest film. Its plot lines featured prostitution, premarital sex, venereal disease, caesarean birth, and a gruesome face-lift operation. Joseph Breen condemned it as the most disgusting film he had ever seen and not only refused it a seal, but tried to have Esper imprisoned for making it.

**Soiled** (1924)
US 41 × 27 in. (104 × 69 cm)
Courtesy of the Tony Nourmand Collection

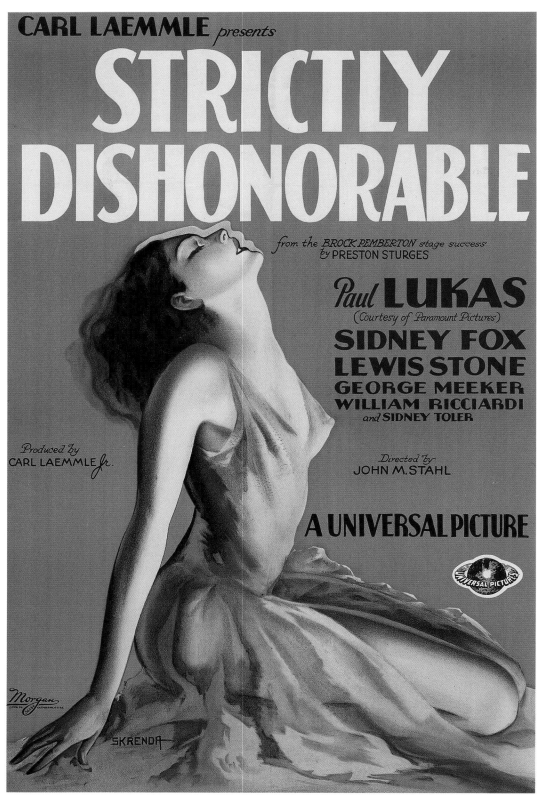

**Strictly Dishonorable** (1931)
US 41 × 27 in. (104 × 69 cm)
Art by Alfred G. Skrenda

Before the introduction of the photographic film poster, illustrations of the cast, particularly the female stars, played a crucial part in attracting audiences. The design that **Alfred G. Skrenda** (1897–1978) created for *Strictly Dishonorable* and the artwork for *The Sin Of Nora Moran* (attributed to **Alberto Vargas** (1896–1982)) demonstrate this beautifully; both simmer with sensuality.

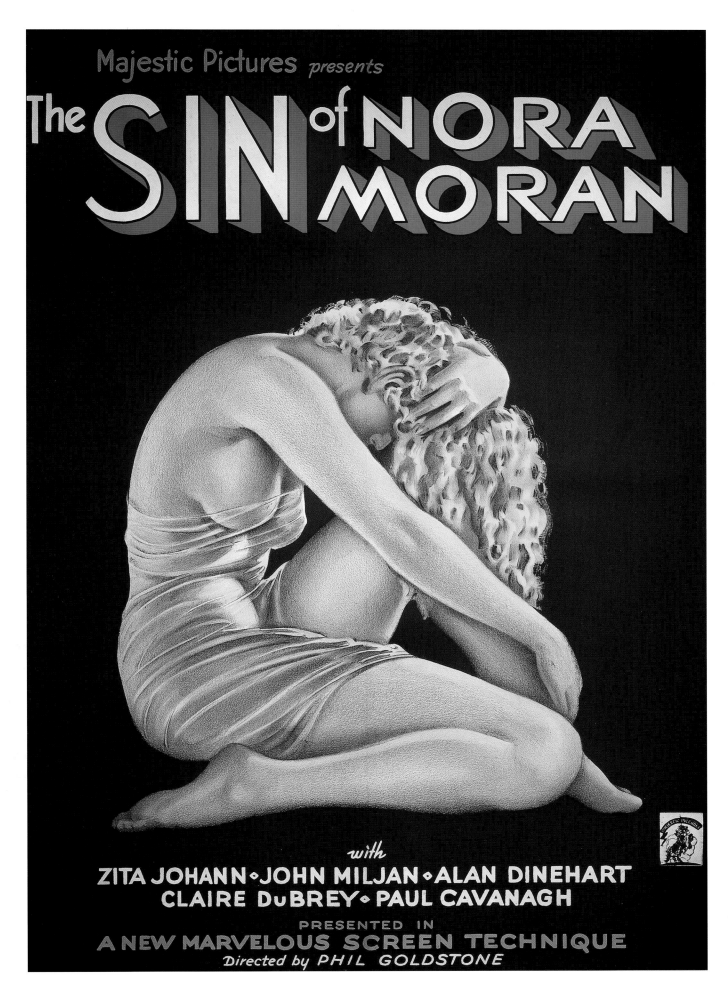

**The Sin Of Nora Moran** (1933)
US 41 × 27 in. (104 × 69 cm)
Art attributed to Alberto Vargas

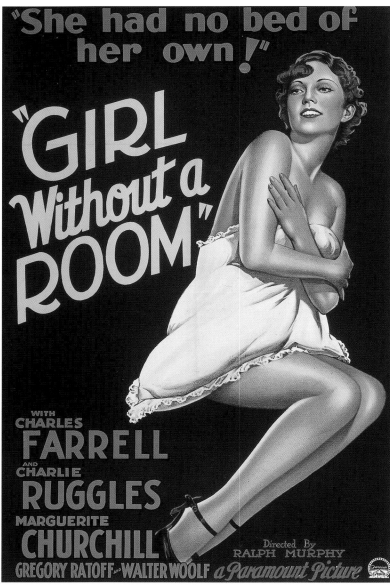

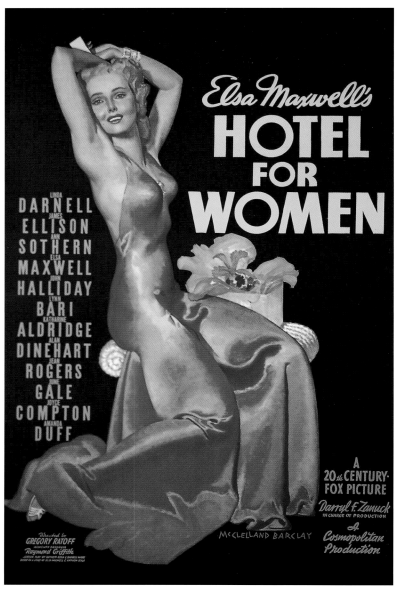

**Girl Without A Room** (1933)
US 41 × 27 in. (104 × 69 cm)
(Style A)
Art direction by Vincent Trotta and Maurice Kallis
Courtesy of the Greg Ferland Collection

**Hotel For Women** (1939)
US 41 × 27 in. (104 × 69 cm)
Art by McClelland Barclay
Courtesy of the Tony Nourmand Collection

Continuing the fashion of using posters to display its leading ladies to the best possible advantage, Twentieth Century Fox hired four eminent illustrators to design four different posters for its *Hotel For Women* campaign. The artists selected were Alberto Vargas, John LaGatta, Bradshaw Crandell and McClelland Barclay and each signed his work; a rare exception to the studios' usual practice of insisting that artists work anonymously and without proper credits.

**McClelland Barclay** (1891–1943) was an accomplished artist, proficient in sculpture, painting, jewellery design and illustration. Most famous for his depictions of beautiful women for the General Motors *Body By Fisher* advertising poster series in the 20s and 30s, he also illustrated several magazine covers, for *Cosmopolitan* and *The Saturday Evening Post* amongst others. During the Second World War, he served in the Navy and designed a number of military poster campaigns and illustrations. Killed in action in 1943, Barclay was awarded the Art Directors Club Medal posthumously in 1944.

Barclay's artwork for *Hotel For Women* is striking and suggestive, yet his imagery is somehow less provocative than that of the pre-Hays *Girl Without A Room* poster, featuring Marguerite Churchill, clearly naked, but tantalisingly concealing a minimal amount of flesh with her pillow. The equally suggestive tagline was a forerunner of the screaming sensationalism of the exploitation industry posters of the later 30s.

Renowned for his glamorous portraits of pin-up girls and paintings of the female nude, Vargas was an obvious choice as artist for *Ladies They Talk About*. He had learnt his craft working as the exclusive artist for the Ziegfeld Follies in the 20s.

**Ladies They Talk About** (1933)
US 41 × 27 in. (104 × 69 cm)
Art by Alberto Vargas
Courtesy of the Wayne Joseph Collection

**Those Three French Girls** (1930)
US 41 × 27 in. (104 × 69 cm)
Courtesy of the Tony Nourmand Collection

The stock market crash of October 1929 plunged America into a devastating Depression. By 1933, the deteriorating economic climate had forced 11,000 of the United States' 25,000 banks to close down and 25–30% of the population were unemployed. That Hollywood managed to survive the depression era largely unscathed was largely due to the fact that its products offered the suffering population a rare opportunity to escape, if only for a couple of hours, from the reality of their situation. Nevertheless, the major studios were all-too-aware of the need to use every means available to them to retain their audiences and during the four years from 1930 to 1934 they exploited sex and innuendo on an unprecedented scale – in the films themselves, in their choice of titles and on the posters that promoted their wares. According to *Variety*, between 1932 and 1933, 352 films out of 440 had 'some sex slant'. In this period Warner Brothers had a deliberate policy of using sex and vice to spice up their product.

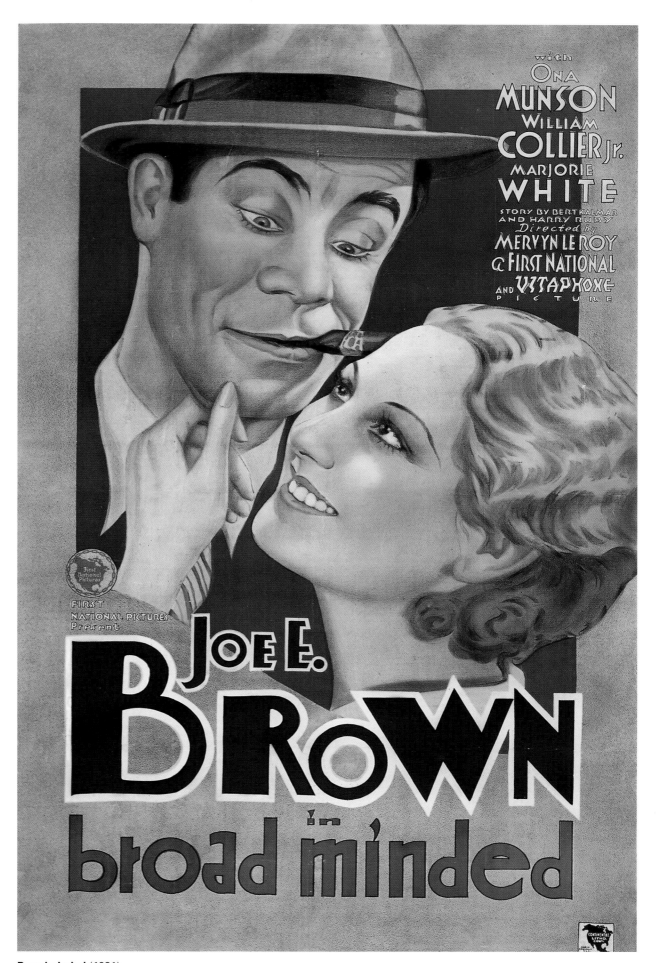

**Broadminded** (1931)
US 41 × 27 in. (104 × 69 cm)
(Style B)
Courtesy of the Tony Nourmand Collection

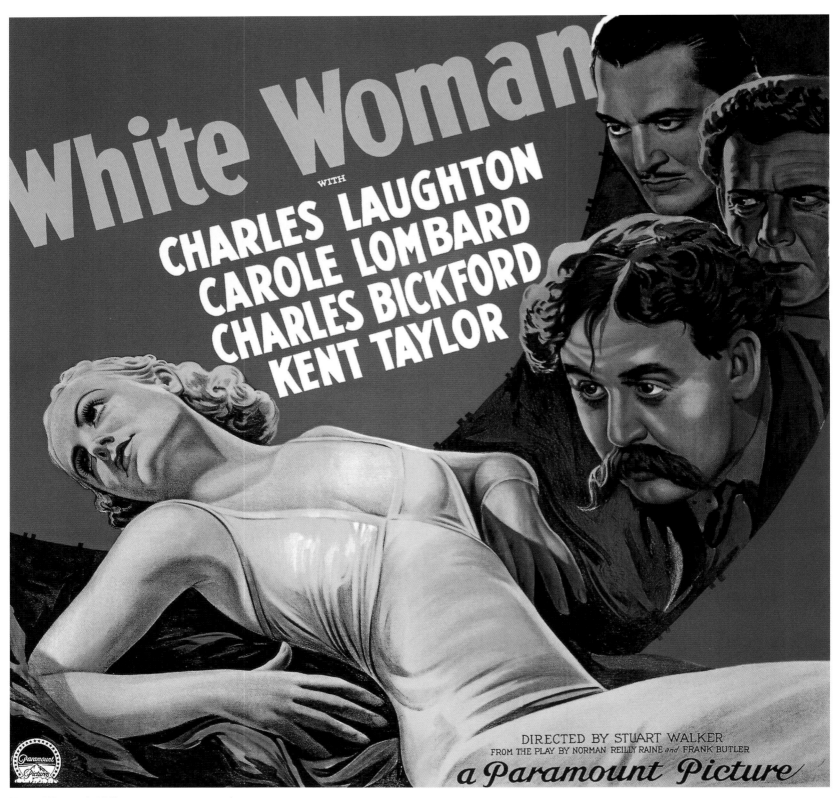

**White Woman** (1933)
US 81 × 81 in. (206 × 206 cm)
Courtesy of the Philip Masheter Collection

*The Bitter Tea Of General Yen* and *White Woman* both dealt with the topic of inter-racial relationships. *Bitter Tea* was Columbia's most expensive production to date and starred Barbara Stanwyck in the leading role of Megan Davis. Its story is basically that of a love affair between Davis and a Chinese General, the latter emerging as the hero of the piece. This was exactly the sort of plot-line that the Hays Office sought to ban and which, after 1934, was relegated to the realms of exploitation. The poster art for both *Bitter Tea* and *White Woman* illustrates the freedom of expression that existed in the pre-Hays era: only a year after the films were released, it was unthinkable for mainstream posters to feature such sensual imagery.

**The Bitter Tea Of General Yen** (1933)
US 41 × 27 in. (104 × 69 cm)

**Tarzan And His Mate** (1934)
US 41 × 27 in. (104 × 69 cm)
(Style C)
Art by William Galbraith Crawford
Courtesy of the Tony Nourmand Collection

Tarzan made his first appearance in *All-Story* magazine in 1912 and was the brainchild of **Edgar Rice Burroughs** (1875–1950). A poor and frustrated salesman, Burroughs turned to writing pulp novels in order to support his family. It proved to be a hugely successful decision, but although Burroughs created a number of other heroes, it is to the vine-swinging 'Man of the Jungle' that he owed his subsequent fame and fortune.

Tarzan first appeared on screen in 1918 but it was Johnny Weissmuller who made the role his own in the classic 1932 hit, *Tarzan The Ape Man*. An Olympic swimming champion, Weissmuller was still relatively unknown as an actor at the time and the poster made no attempt to capture his true likeness – instead Tarzan's appearance is modelled on the character from the original books. By the time *Tarzan And His Mate* was released two years later, the actor was so well-known that it was necessary to produce a more accurate portrait.

*Tarzan And His Mate*, which is considered the best in the Tarzan series, was also the most controversial. The complete, uncensored version of the film featured full-frontal female nudity in a scene where Tarzan and Jane swim underwater (the film's female star, Maureen O'Sullivan, was replaced by an Olympic swimmer body-double). Although the film had been made before the Hays Code was rigorously enforced, the film did still have to pass the industry censorship board and the underwater scene was deemed improper. The film therefore has the dubious honour of being the first to lose an appeal against Breen and the Production Code Administration office. It was an ominous foretaste of the rigid censorship which would be imposed on Hollywood for the next third of a century. Despite the ruling, MGM still circulated a few unedited prints of the film and a number of trailers still contained the nude scene.

*Flesh And The Devil* was another risqué MGM venture and featured erotic and sensual love scenes between Greta Garbo and John Gilbert. It was one of Garbo's earliest films and the first time she had been paired with Gilbert. The couple were having an affair in real life and this only added to their on-screen chemistry. *Flesh And The Devil* broke box office records on its release.

**William Galbraith Crawford** (1894–1978) had a prolific career in illustration. He designed book jackets and illustrated several covers for *The New Yorker*. He also worked on numerous posters for MGM throughout the 20s and 30s and his work remains some of the most collectable of the era.

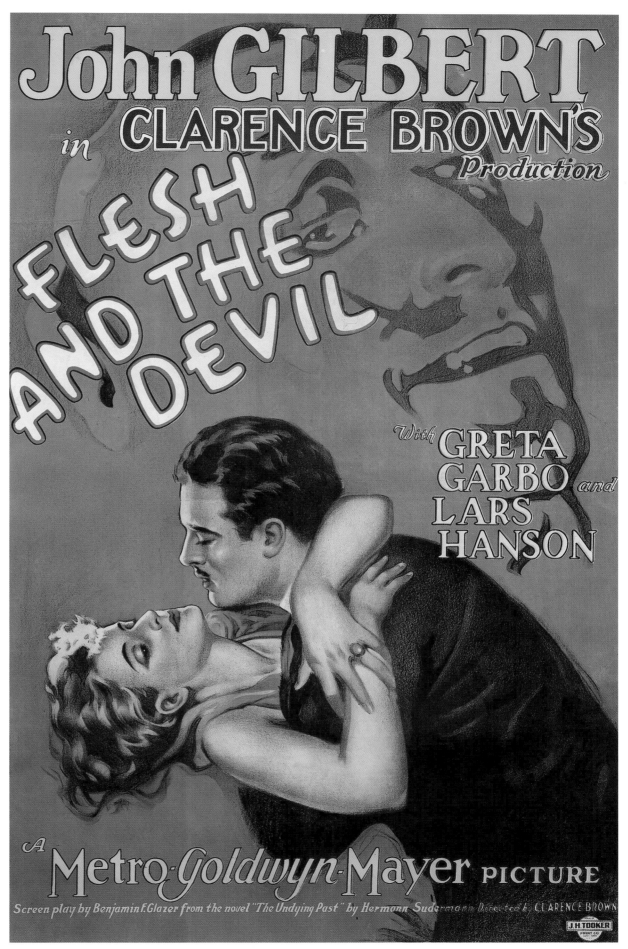

**Flesh And The Devil** (1926)
US 41 × 27 in. (104 × 69 cm)
Art attributed to William Galbraith Crawford
Courtesy of the Andrew Cohen Collection

**Cock Of The Air** (1932)
US 41 × 27 in. (104 × 69 cm)
Art attributed to Alvan Cordell 'Hap' Hadley
Courtesy of the Tony Nourmand Collection

**Alvan Cordell 'Hap' Hadley** (1895–1976) is recognized as one of the most adventurous and influential poster artists of his era. As was the case with many of his contemporaries, Hadley began his career during the First World War when he was one of the Marine Corps' official artists. He later owned his own advertising studio in Manhattan where he produced work for all the major film studios over a period of more than thirty years. Primarily renowned for designing Charlie Chaplin and Buster Keaton film posters, Hadley's art also adorns the posters for many Howard Hughes productions.

**Howard Hughes** (1905–1976) was a man of many faces; a shrewd businessman, aviator, womanizer and movie mogul, he was a flamboyant figure in the Hollywood of the 30s and early 40s. Later in life, however, he suffered from mental instability and became a notorious recluse.

Hughes, who had inherited a vast fortune, formed his own aircraft company in 1932 and was a pioneer in designing and building his own planes. By 1938, he had broken most of the world's aviation records and would go on to build the world's largest airplane, the famous 'Spruce Goose'. His production of *Hell's Angels* (1930) allowed him to combine his enthusiasm for aviation with movie-making. It was the most expensive movie of its time, and featured large numbers of WW1 warplanes in dramatic flying sequences. Although not quite on the same scale, aviation was also the theme of *Cock Of The Air*, as shown on 'Hap' Hadley's caricature illustration for the film's poster.

Hughes brought the same enthusiasm to the pursuit of beautiful women as he did to building planes and making films. He is reputed to have had affairs with most of the leading ladies in contemporary Hollywood, including Katherine Hepburn, Jean Harlow, Bette Davis and Ava Gardner. For *The Outlaw* he used his engineering expertise to create a prototype of the push-up bra in a (surely unnecessary) attempt to accentuate Jane Russell's bust. Russell's cleavage, liberally displayed, was a major *motif* in the film, and even more so in the advertising campaign, and brought Hughes into serious conflict with the censors. The director anticipated trouble from the Production Code Administration in advance, and thus attempted to release the film under his own steam. He premiered the film in San Francisco with an accompanying poster declaring 'The picture that couldn't be stopped!' Joseph Breen had other ideas, however, and withdrew the picture from circulation. It did not receive an official seal until 1950. More than sixty years on, the film still manages to create a stir. When the premiere poster (from Hughes original release in 1943 in San Francisco) surfaced in an auction at Christie's London in March 2003, it broke all previous European movie poster records, selling for £52,875 ($95,000), and the sale made front-page headlines in newspapers across the UK.

**The Outlaw** (1943)
US 81 × 81 in. (206 × 206 cm)
Courtesy of the Tarek AbuZayyad Collection

I'm not bad,
I'm just drawn
that way.

**Who Framed Roger Rabbit?** (1988)
US 41 × 27 in. (104 × 69 cm)
(Style E)
Licensed Limited Edition by Kilian Enterprises
Design by Dayna Stedry
Illustration by 22/63 Graphics
Courtesy of the Martin Bridgewater Collection

Although both fairly tame Disney films, *Dick Tracy* and *Who Framed Roger Rabbit?* were marketed with a stress on the well-established exploitation themes of sex and innuendo. The real-life affair between Madonna and Warren Beatty, the stars of *Dick Tracy*, gave a fillip to the campaign. It also imbued the Advance (Madonna) poster with sexual undertones that were deliberately highlighted by an audacious tagline. Ultimately, the poster was judged just a little too risqué for the family-oriented studio and was withdrawn from circulation.

For *Who Framed Roger Rabbit?*, Disney produced two limited-edition mylar posters featuring Jessica Rabbit in glamour photo poses.

"Mind If I Call You Dick?"

**Dick Tracy** (1990)
US 41 × 27 in. (104 × 69 cm)
(Advance – Madonna (Withdrawn))
Art by Johnny Kwan
Courtesy of the Tony Nourmand Collection

**The Whip Woman** (1928)
US 41 × 27 in. (104 × 69 cm)
Courtesy of the Haldane Collection

**Allen Jones** (b. 1937) is a renowned painter, printmaker and sculptor. He has won numerous awards for his work, which has been exhibited worldwide. Jones was a key figure in an influential movement that helped redefine British art by embracing unconventional and irreverent ideas and looking to popular culture for its inspiration. Jones is famous for his portrayal of beautiful women and the poster for *Maîtresse* illustrates this aspect of his work. His style is characterized by a striking and bold use of colour combined with a unique painting technique.

GERARD DEPARDIEU

BULLE OGIER

A LOVE STORY ABOUT    THE MYSTERIES OF LOVE

She will open your eyes.

A film by
Barbet SCHROEDER

No one under 17 admitted.
Distributed by Tinc Productions Corp.

**Maîtresse** (1973)
US 41 × 27 in. (104 × 69 cm)
Art by Allen Jones
Courtesy of the Tony Nourmand Collection

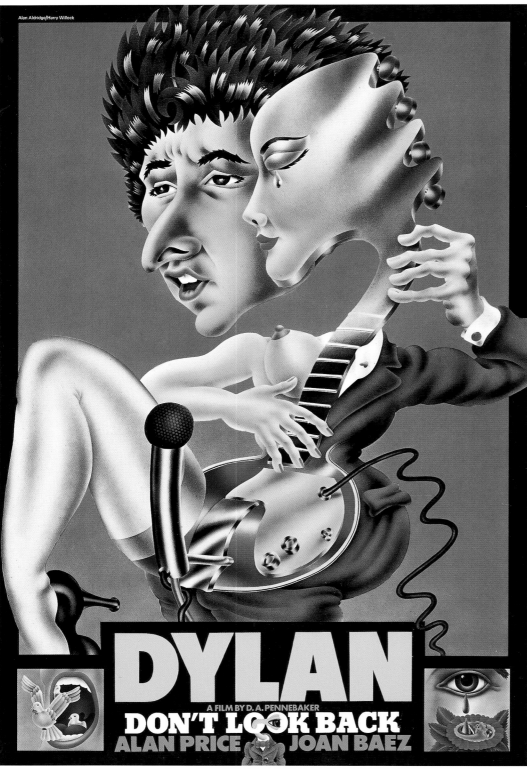

**Don't Look Back** (1967)
British 30 × 20 in. (76 × 51 cm)
Art by Alan Aldridge and Harry Willock
Courtesy of the Tony Nourmand Collection

The award-winning **Alan Aldridge** (b. 1937) was one of the most famous and important graphic designers of the 60s. A self-taught artist who left school at fifteen, he developed a distinctive, rich style that quickly found favour with the London set. His work, reflecting the psychedelic and experimental spirit of the age, was admired and embraced by bands like The Beatles, The Rolling Stones, The Who and Pink Floyd, for whom he designed various album covers. His artwork for *Don't Look Back* perfectly illustrates his unique and highly effective style. In 1963 he was hired by Penguin Books as the Art Director of their fiction list. In this role Aldridge was instrumental in re-vamping the publisher's image by abandoning its traditional typographical cover designs in favour of bold and bright graphics.

With such talent, and as a friend of Andy Warhol, Aldridge was an obvious choice as designer for the British poster for Warhol's film *Chelsea Girls*, and this remains one of his most famous works. Although the image won a Silver Award from The Design and Art Director's Club, the censors remained unimpressed and the fly-posting of the poster across London led to Aldridge's prosecution.

*Chelsea Girls* was one of the first 'underground' films to break into mainstream cinema and although banned in Boston and Chicago, it was a critical success in London, New York and San Francisco.

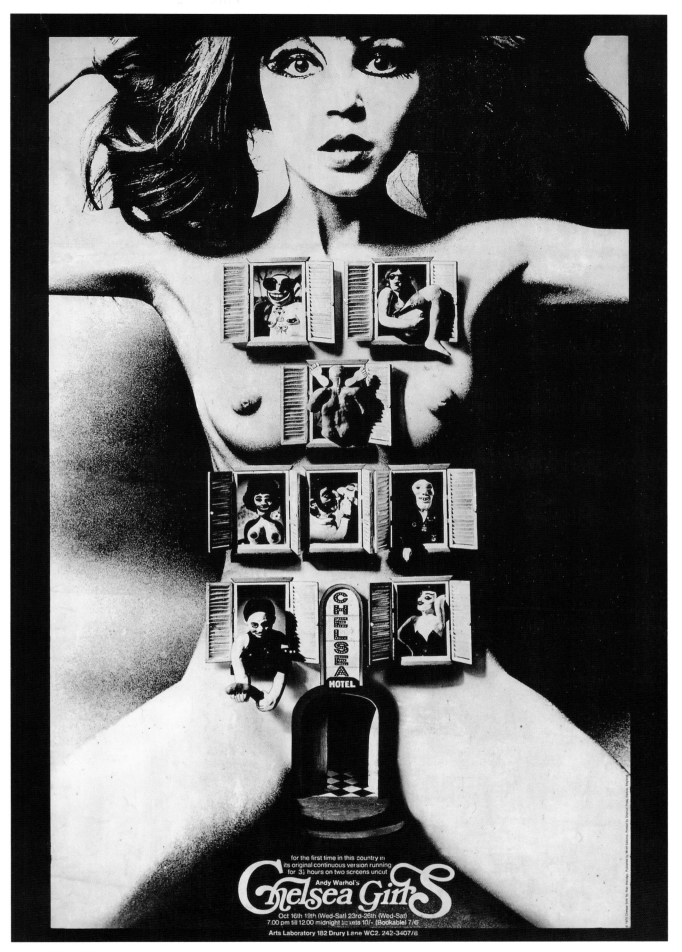

**Chelsea Girls** (1966)
British 30 × 20 in. (76 × 51 cm)
Art by Alan Aldridge
Courtesy of the Tony Nourmand Collection

**Acid – Delirio Dei Sensi** (1968)
Italian 39 × 108 in. (99 × 274 cm)
Courtesy of the Philip Shalam Collection

In the 60s, shrewd producers quickly realized that, given the free-spirited mood of the times, there was a big demand for films featuring the wonders of recreational drugs. They churned out countless low-budget, poor quality movies that targeted a young and apparently insatiable audience. *Acid – Delirio Dei Sensi* was one such offering from Italy and although the film itself was less than brilliant, its promotional art was phenomenal. The banner poster is a particularly dazzling example of Italian design: a brilliantly crafted, sensual illustration of a naked woman painted tattoo-like from head to toe, surmounted by typography evocative of the drug's effect. This image has become almost iconic, although the film itself has been long forgotten.

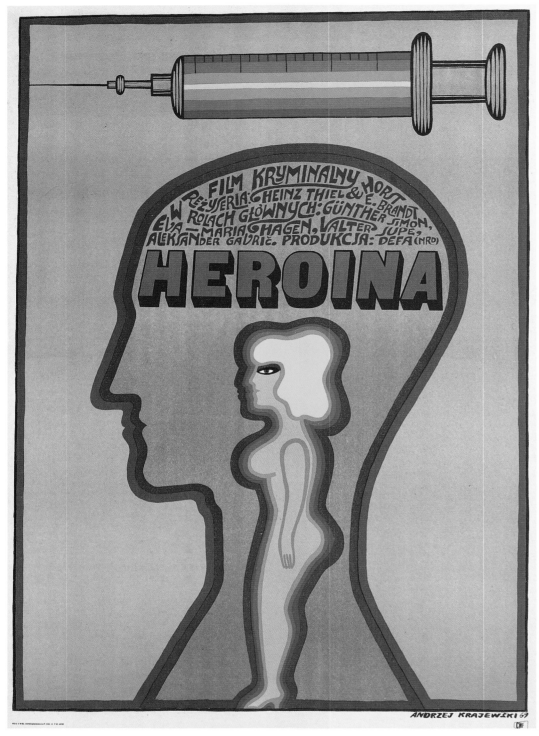

Based on the play *The Addicts*, *Way Out* is the story of a group of youngsters who find their way out of drug addiction through turning to Christ. Directed by a Congregational Minister, Irvin S. Yeaworth Jr., the film carries a strong Christian message and was made primarily for use as an evangelistic tool. Yeaworth is better known for his science fiction films, especially the cult classic, *The Blob* (1958). The graphic simplicity of the poster for *Way Out* powerfully evokes the painful dilemma of the addict.

**Heroin (Heroina)** (1968)
Polish 33 × 23 in. (84 × 58 cm)
Art by Andrzej Krajewski
Courtesy of the Tomoaki 'Nigo' Nagao Collection

**Andrzej Krajewski** (b. 1933) is famous for his work in the 60s and 70s that embodied the counter-culture movement of the period. His artwork for *Heroin* is a perfect example of his colourful, bold style. Krajewski has won numerous awards worldwide for his art.

A PREMIERE PRESENTATION
IN WIDE SCREEN COLOR

# WAY OUT

THE WILD WORLD OF THE DRUG ADDICT

more than a movie...an experience
real life addicts portray today's
youth going WAY OUT for kicks.

screenplay by Jean Yeaworth and Rudy & Shirley Nelson, based upon "The Addicts" by John Gimenez
music by Kurt Kaiser, produced and directed by Irvin S. Yeaworth, Jr,. a Valley Forge film

**Way Out** (1967)
US 41 × 27 in. (104 × 69 cm)
(Premiere)
Courtesy of the Tony Nourmand Collection

**The Weird World Of LSD** (1967)
US 36 × 25 in. (91 × 64 cm)
(Style A)
Courtesy of the Tony Nourmand Collection

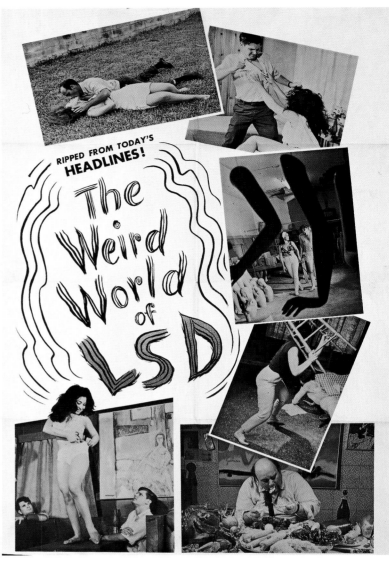

**The Weird World Of LSD** (1967)
US 36 × 25 in. (91 × 64 cm)
(Style B)
Courtesy of the Tony Nourmand Collection

● **1943**. LSD is synthesized for the first time by Swiss scientist Albert Hoffman.

LSD was the *drug de jour* in the 60s and played a major role in the counter-culture movement of the decade. Very little was known about the drug at first, a point that the exploitation industry was quick to seize upon, capitalizing on the widespread ignorance to sell films like *Hallucination Generation* and *The Weird World Of LSD*. The latter was strikingly reminiscent of the 30s drug menace films, the main difference being the substitution of LSD for marijuana.

# TONIGHT
## YOU ARE INVITED TO A 'PILL PARTY'

You will experience every jolt…every jar of a Psychedelic Circus…The Beatniks…Sickniks… and Acid-Heads…and you will witness their ecstasies, their agonies and their bizarre sensualities…You will be hurled into their debauched dreams and frenzied fantasies!

FOR THE ADULT MINDED…

the revealing story of today's…

## HALLUCINATION GENERATION

STARRING GEORGE **MONTGOMERY** · DANNY **STONE** ·

Herbert R. Steinmann Presents
An Edward Mann · Robert D. Weinbach Production
Produced by NIGEL COX · Written and Directed by EDWARD MANN
A TRANS AMERICAN RELEASE

Copyright ©1966  Trans American Films  Printed in U.S.A.

**Hallucination Generation** (1966)
US 41 × 27 in. (104 × 69 cm)
Courtesy of the Tony Nourmand Collection

**The Trip** (1968)
US 41 × 27 in. (104 × 69 cm)
Courtesy of the Tony Nourmand Collection

**Psych-Out** (1968)
US 41 × 27 in. (104 × 69 cm)
Courtesy of the Tony Nourmand Collection

Released in 1968, *The Trip* provides a stark contrast to the scare-mongering sensationalism of *The Weird World Of LSD*. Written by Jack Nicholson, it is, in effect, an 85-minute LSD trip. Director Roger Corman reportedly took acid in order to research the subject. The film was instantly condemned for trying to exploit the LSD phenomenon and for what was, some claimed, its pro-drug stance. A year after *The Trip* was released, the Production Code ceased to exist. *Psych-Out* and *The Acid Eaters* are two more examples of the increasingly glamorous way in which drugs were presented in 60s cinema.

**The Acid Eaters** (1967)
US 41 × 27 in. (104 × 69 cm)
Courtesy of the Tony Nourmand Collection

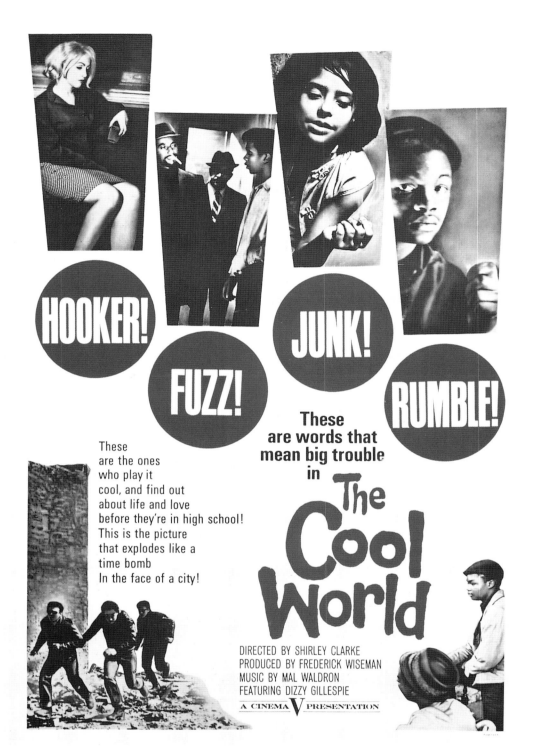

**The Cool World** (1966)
US 41 × 27 in. (104 × 69 cm)
Courtesy of the Tony Nourmand Collection

**Shirley Clarke** (1919–1997) was a key player in the campaign to develop an alternative, *avant-garde* approach to filmmaking in the 50s and 60s. Starting out as a dancer and choreographer, Clarke began her directing career in 1953 and became the only female member of a group established to advance the cause of independent films. This group rejected the commercial cinema of the day, believing it to be corrupt, morally questionable and artistically weak. When she released *The Connection* in 1962, it won a special award at the Cannes Film Festival. It was also banned by the New York State Censorship Board and became a test case for the freedom of expression.

*The Cool World* was also a *tour-de-force*, and was an unflinching and gritty record of life in Harlem. It was the first independent film to play at the Venice Film Festival and helped pioneer the docu-drama genre.

*More* was another 60s film that took an alternative approach. Directed by **Barbet Schroeder** (b. 1941) it detailed a man's descent into heroin addiction. Schroeder was a disciple of the *Nouvelle Vague* movement in France and had worked with directors like Jean Luc-Goddard. *More* is infused with the same spirit as the films of the French 'New Wave' and was a hit in Europe. Played to a soundtrack by Pink Floyd, the film has become a cult classic.

**More** (1969)
US 41 × 27 in. (104 × 69 cm)
Photo by Lester Waldman
Courtesy of the Simon Tapson Collection

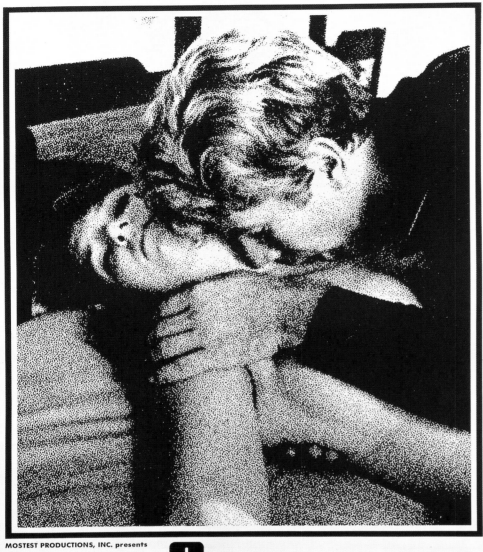

MOSTEST PRODUCTIONS, INC. presents

# A TASTE OF FLESH

...the intimate embraces
of lovemaking's most provocative acts!

**A Taste Of Her Flesh (A Taste Of Flesh)** (1967)
US 41 × 27 in. (104 × 69 cm)
Courtesy of The X-rated Collection

Although also a female filmmaker in the 60s, the work of **Doris Wishman** (1912–2002) was worlds away, in terms of both content and style, from that of Shirley Clarke. Wishman, who made over thirty exploitation films over the course of her career, helped pioneer the 'roughie' genre. The plots were crazy and far-fetched, the budgets non-existent and the acting minimal; but Wishman's films were a hit in an industry where none of these things mattered, so long as nudity, sex and violence were ever-present. This said, Wishman did have certain talents. She was the only woman in a male-dominated industry and was a sound, honest businesswoman. She wrote, directed and edited the films herself and the filmmaking techniques and camera angles she used were often surprisingly experimental and artistic. The extra depth and originality of her work proved to be inspiring both within and beyond the exploitation industry. Wishman's films influenced the work of directors like John Waters, Roger Corman and John Carpenter.

A
DORIS
WISHMAN
PRODUCTION

# BAD
# GIRLS
# GO TO
# HELL

A JURI
PICTURES
RELEASE

**Bad Girls Go To Hell** (1965)
US 41 × 27 in. (104 × 69 cm)
(Colour Version)
Courtesy of the Tony Nourmand Collection

**The Beatniks** (1959)
US 41 × 27 in. (104 × 69 cm)
Courtesy of the Tony Nourmand Collection

America in the 50s was a nation plagued by contradictions. Enjoying unprecedented affluence, the white middle-classes had the freedom to spend and consume as never before, but this privilege was not shared by most minority groups, particularly African-Americans, who were left to continue their struggle against prejudice and poverty. Even among those who were free to enjoy the steady rise in prosperity there were a few who felt that the price to be paid in terms of the increasing blandness and conformity of American society, was too heavy. For many creative artists, including filmmakers, the political witch-hunts instigated by Senator Joseph McCarthy also cast a heavy shadow over the decade.

A number of writers and artists, including Edward Hopper, Arthur Miller and Tennessee Williams began to speak out against what they saw as a repressive and hypocritical society. Their words gave inspiration and encouragement to an even more rebellious group of 'angry young men' who became known as the Beatniks – men like Jack Kerouac, Allen Ginsberg and William Burroughs lived by their own rules and embraced a freedom that the prevailing culture could neither offer nor tolerate. The socio-cultural impact of the Beatniks was immense and enduring: the spirit that they embodied would become the defining ethos of the 60s.

As outsiders, the Beats experienced all the usual stereotyping and prejudice from those around them. Never slow to spot an opportunity, the exploitation film industry was quick to take advantage of the public's ignorance and disapproval of what *Time* magazine called 'a pack of oddballs who celebrate dope, sex and despair'. Films like *The Beatniks* presented the Beat Generation as nothing more than a lawless bunch of troublemakers.

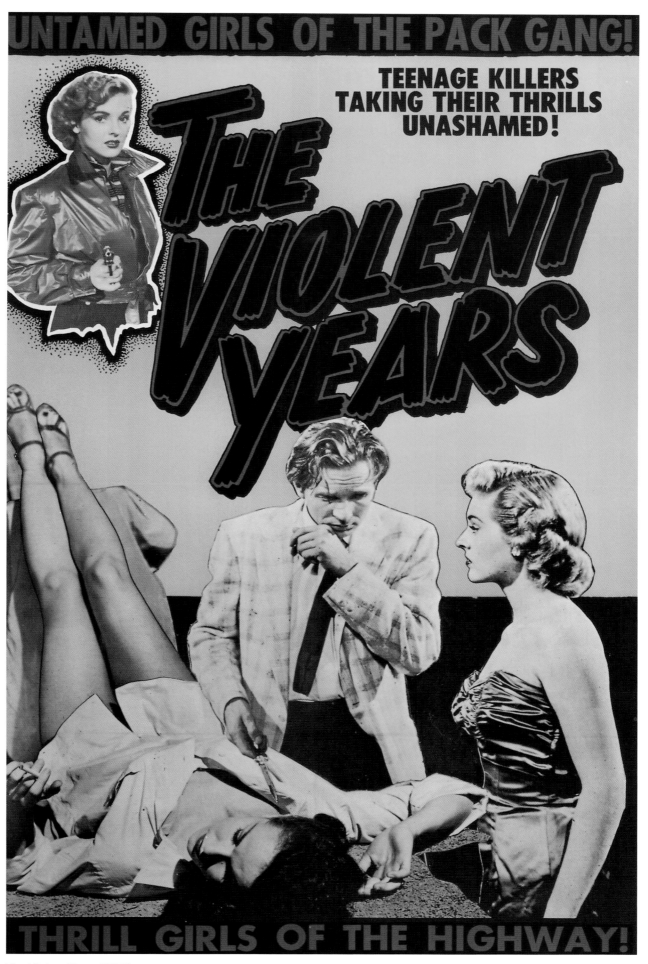

**The Violent Years** (1956)
US 41 × 27 in. (104 × 69 cm)
Courtesy of the Tony Nourmand Collection

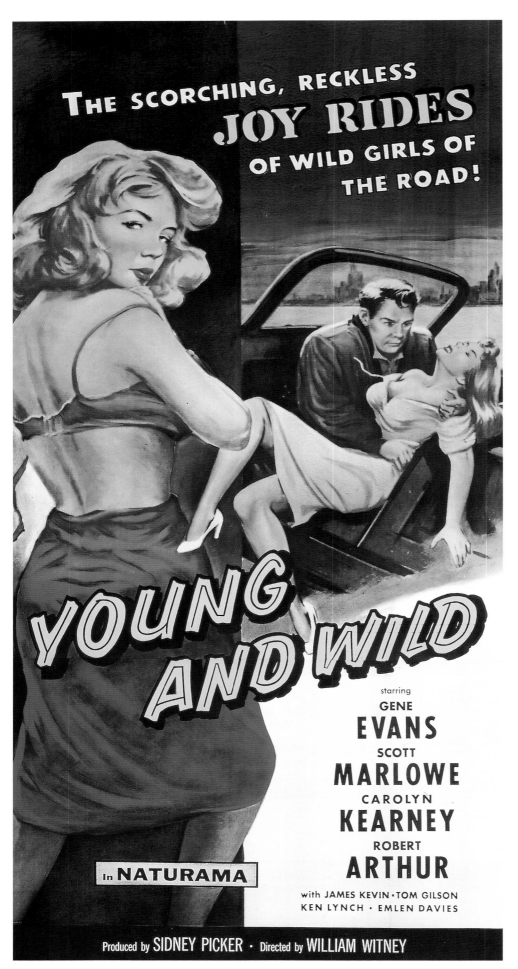

**Young And Wild** (1958)
US 81 × 41 in. (206 × 104 cm)
Courtesy of the Tony Nourmand Collection

The makers of 50s exploitation and 'B' movies conveniently simplified the Beat phenomenon and grouped its supporters, along with juvenile delinquents, under the general heading of rebellious teenagers. Teenage rebels, especially if they were male, were depicted on-screen as a threat to everything middle America held dear – especially its daughters. Often the focus of such films was the age-old 'good girl gone bad' plot that saw sweet, promising young women turn into 'wild gals' under the influence of the rock 'n' roll, Beat Generation.

**Live Fast, Die Young** (1958)
US 41 × 27 in. (104 × 69 cm)
Courtesy of the Tony Nourmand Collection

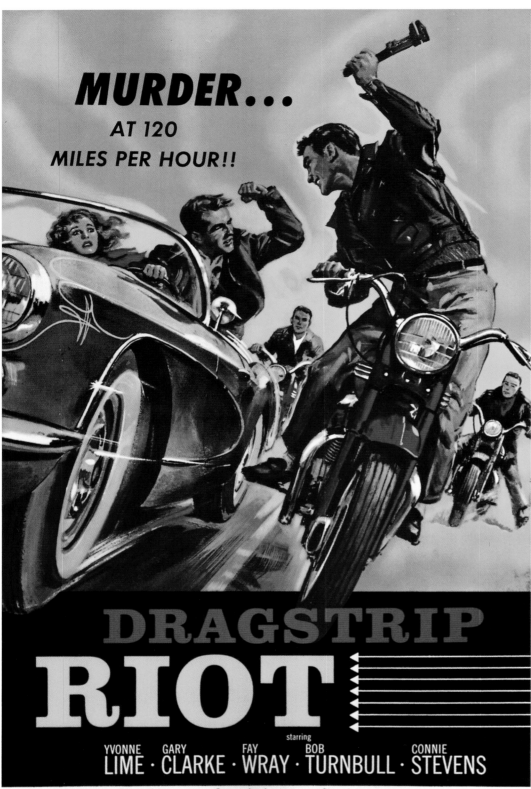

**Dragstrip Riot** (1958)
US 41 × 27 in. (104 × 69 cm)
Courtesy of the Haldane Collection

Hot cars, hot girls, hot music and glowering, independent teens were the key ingredients of the sub-genre of 'Hot Rod' films that emerged during the 50s. By the middle of the decade, Hot Rod movies were being made at a rate of about one a week and they played to drive-in audiences.

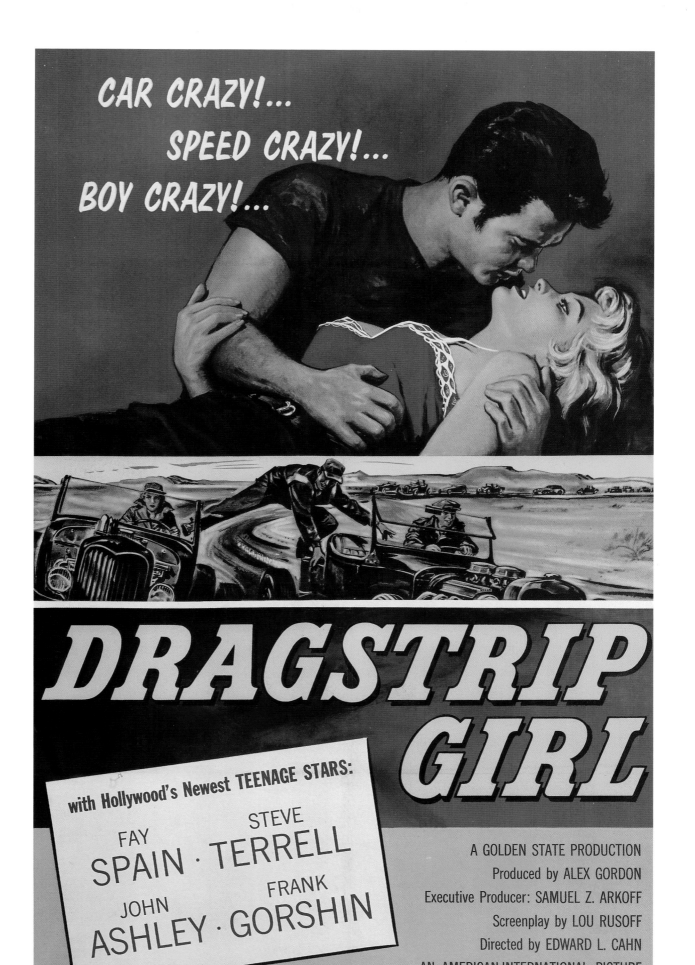

**Dragstrip Girl** (1957)
US 41 × 27 in. (104 × 69 cm)
Courtesy of the Tony Nourmand Collection

**Hot Rod Gang** (1958)
US 81 × 41 in. (206 × 104 cm)
Courtesy of the Tony Nourmand Collection

Hot Rod films were made on low budgets and featured unknown actors, for it was the car, not the plot or the characters, that was the centrepiece of the show. The genre continued to develop well into the 60s and 70s and spawned cult classics such as *Easy Rider* and *Two Lane Blacktop*.

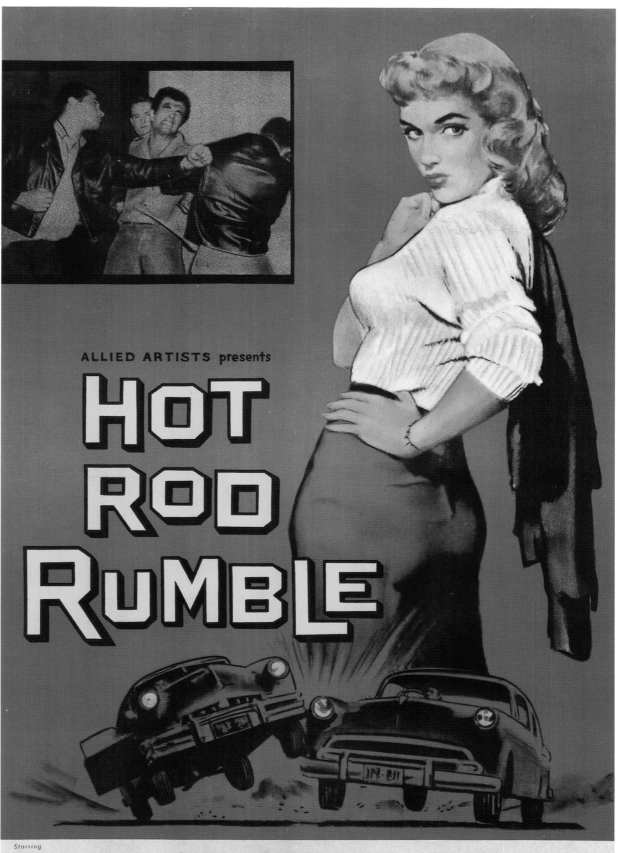

**Hot Rod Rumble** (1957)
US 41 × 27 in. (104 × 69 cm)
Courtesy of the Tony Nourmand Collection

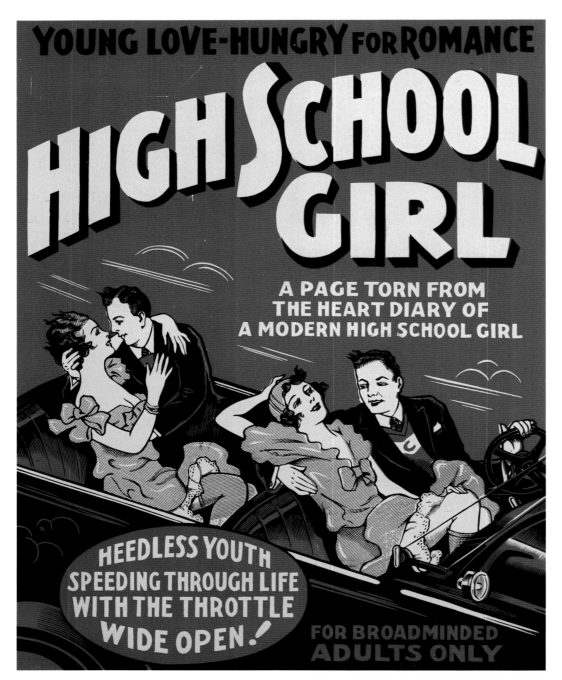

**High School Girl** (1934)
US 41 × 27 in. (104 × 69 cm)
Courtesy of the Tony Nourmand Collection

Made in 1944, *Teen Age* is one of the earliest examples of the use of the terms 'teen-age' or 'teenager' outside specialist literature. Although it had first been coined by a sociologist in the 20s it did not enter common usage until the mid 40s. In the April 1945 issue of *American Speech* it was listed in the 'new words' section, while in 1947 *Encyclopædia Britannica* still identified 'teenager' as a new term.

The origin of the word 'teen' itself can be traced back to the eighth century, when it meant grief, sorrow or misery!

**Teen Age** (1944)
US 41 × 27 in. (104 × 69 cm)
(Style A)
Courtesy of the Otto Buj Collection

**The Flaming Teen-Age** (1956)
US 41 × 27 in. (104 × 69 cm)
Courtesy of the Tony Nourmand Collection

**Sorority Girl** (1957)
US 41 × 27 in. (104 × 69 cm)
Courtesy of the Tony Nourmand Collection

Juvenile delinquency was not an exclusively male phenomenon and the 50s saw a wave of films that featured 'bad girls'. These depicted the usual mix of teen rebellion, lawlessness and sex, but with reckless females as the protagonists. From the 'shock by shock' confessions of the *Sorority Girl* to the 'jailbait' *Runaway Daughters,* the exploitation industry emphasized the perils of letting bad girls out on the loose.

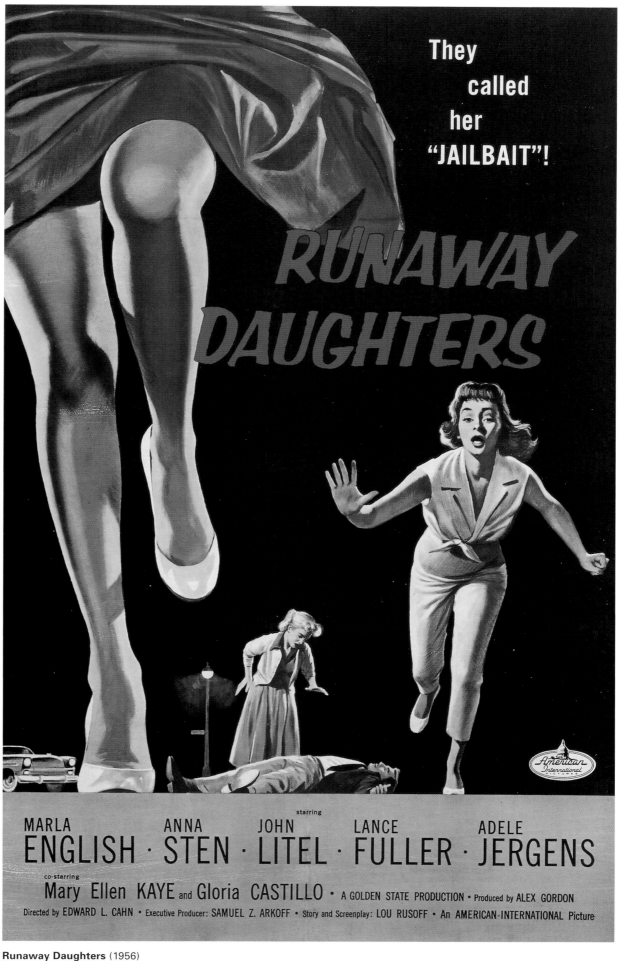

**Runaway Daughters** (1956)
US 41 × 27 in. (104 × 69 cm)
Courtesy of the Tony Nourmand Collection

**High School Hellcats** (1958)
US 41 × 27 in. (104 × 69 cm)
Courtesy of the Tony Nourmand Collection

**Hugo Haas** (1901–1968) was the acknowledged master of bad 'bad girl' flicks. Born in Czechoslovakia, Haas had been a respected character actor in his homeland before being forced to flee in the face of the Nazi invasion. He made his way to America where he began working as an announcer on US broadcasts to occupied Eastern Europe. After the war, he tried to resurrect his acting career but found himself all too frequently typecast as a greasy, foreign villain. Nonetheless, acting did enable Haas to finance his first love: filmmaking. In the 50s, he began churning out his own independent films, which he both starred in and directed. His sensationalist bad girl flicks followed the typical 'B' movie model. All his plots unfolded with the same general storyline: a lonely, middle-aged man (played by Haas) is seduced by a sexy blonde with a bad reputation. *Pickup* was just one in a long line of similar films. Due to a fatally provocative tagline – 'They gave her a bad name and she lived up to it!' – the American poster for *Pickup* was withdrawn from circulation. It was replaced by another with the same image, but this time the slogan read:
'Easy to pick-up'.

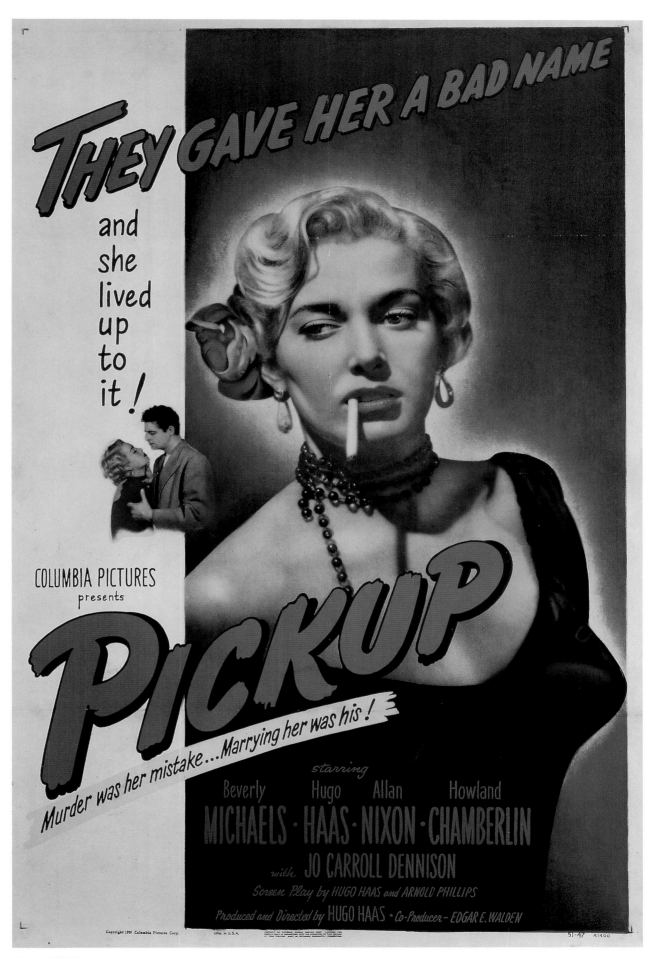

**Pickup** (1951)
US 41 × 27 in. (104 × 69 cm)
(Withdrawn)
Courtesy of the Matthew Daly Collection

**Juvenile Jungle** (1958)
US 22 × 28 in. (56 × 71 cm)
(Style B)
Courtesy of the Tony Nourmand Collection

Before the Second World War, the hopes and expectations of the majority of American 'teenagers' were severely restricted. Money was still tight for most families in the wake of the depression and only a minority of young people could contemplate a college education, so the options for girls were often limited to motherhood and domesticity while boys were still expected to go straight into work. With the post-war affluence of the 50s, however, things began to change. Teenagers received allowances, were given greater free time and college became an option. The result was an independent generation that eagerly embraced the freedoms on offer. This new state of affairs, perhaps inevitably, created growing tensions between children and their parents. Many teenagers rebelled against the orthodoxies of their parents' generation and a new phenomenon was borne: juvenile delinquency. Exploitation cinema was quick to pounce on this trend and films like *Teenage Crime Wave* and *Juvenile Jungle* helped to fuel society's fears that the younger generation was out of control.

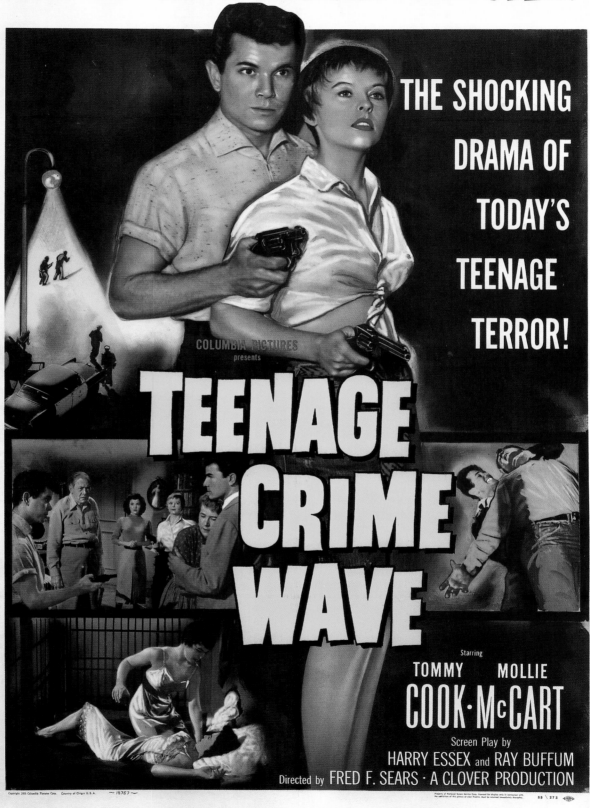

**Teenage Crime Wave** (1955)
US 41 × 27 in. (104 × 69 cm)
Courtesy of the Tony Nourmand Collection

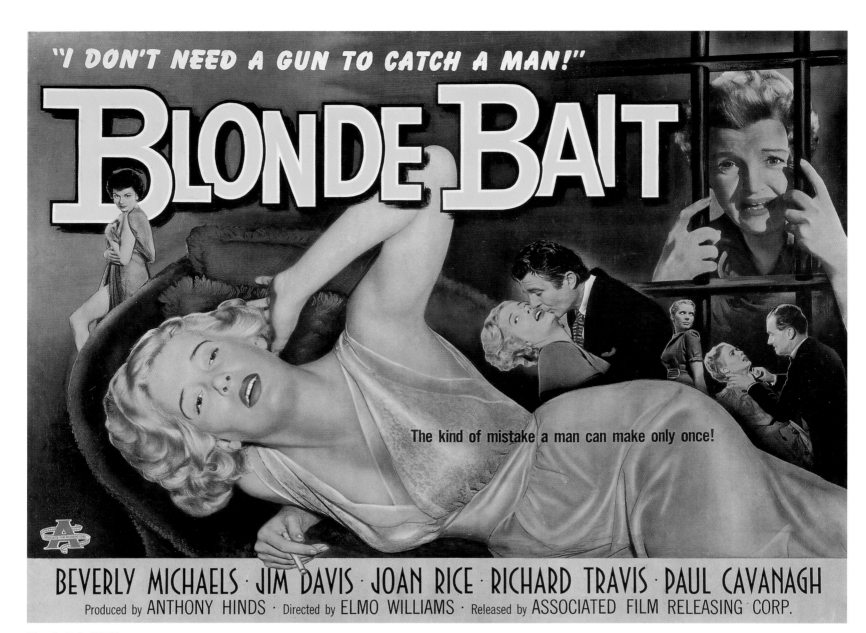

**Blonde Bait** (1956)
US 22 × 28 in. (56 × 71 cm)
Courtesy of the Tony Nourmand Collection

**Beverly Michaels** (b. 1928) and **Peggy Cummins** (b. 1925) were two of the most renowned 'bad girls' of 50s cinema. The careers of both thrived as they starred in the roles of seductive *femmes fatales* in a succession of B-movie flicks. *Blonde Bait* and *Deadly Is The Female* are two examples of the genre; the latter remains one of the most iconic 'B' film noirs of all time. The suggestive US poster for *Deadly Is The Female* exemplifies the classic exploitation techniques that were used to advertise this film, later re-named *Gun Crazy*.

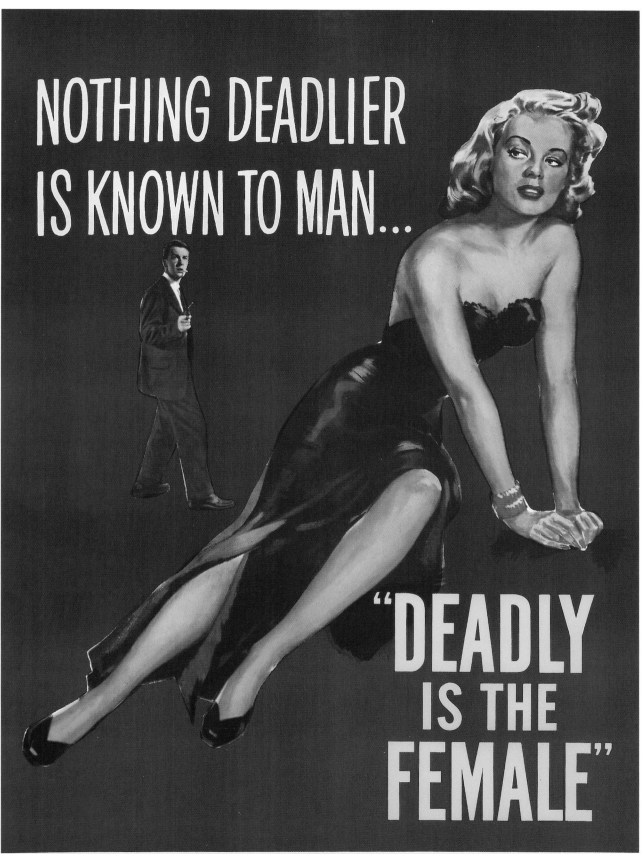

**Deadly Is The Female** (1950)
US 41 × 27 in. (104 × 69 cm)
Courtesy of the Fabyan Daw Collection

**Three Bad Sisters** (1956)
US 22 × 28 in. (56 × 71 cm)
(Style B)
Courtesy of the Tony Nourmand Collection

**Ewald André Dupont** (1891–1956) had a successful film career in his native Germany. By the outbreak of the First World War he had established himself as the country's leading film critic and by 1917 he was directing his own motion pictures. Dupont's most significant and influential works are *Variety* (1925), *Piccadilly* (1929) and the Anglo-American *Atlantic* (1929); the latter is notable for being the first European all-talkie. Unfortunately, like many European directors, Dupont found that his career went into decline following his move to Hollywood. He emigrated in 1933 and soon found himself being consistently assigned to work on low-budget, badly written movies. Increasingly disillusioned, Dupont gave up directing in the 40s to become a talent agent; but by the 50s, he was back directing trashy, drive-in 'B' flicks like *Problem Girls*.

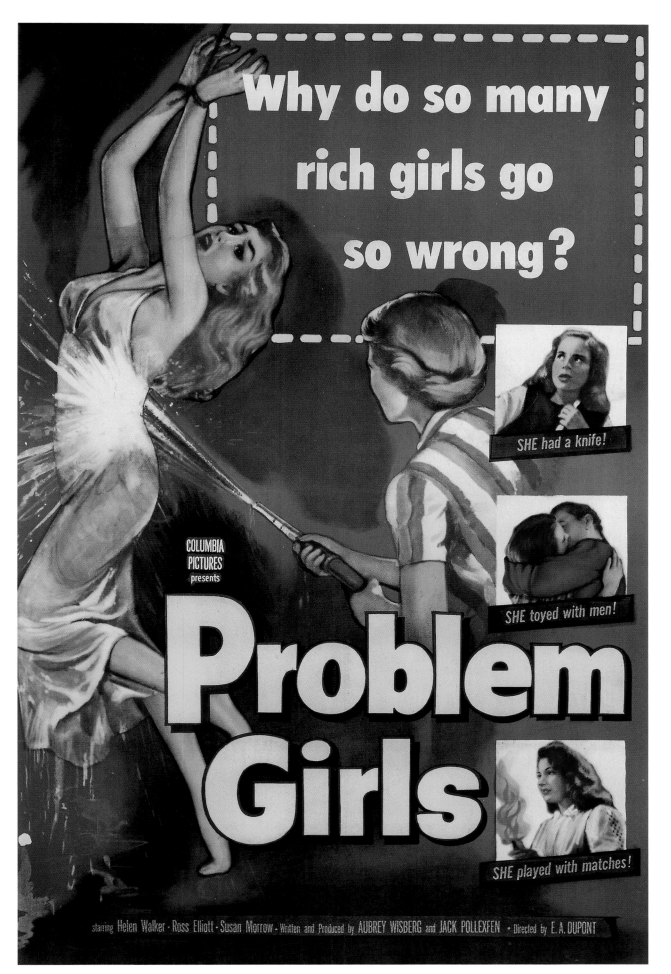

**Problem Girls** (1953)
US 41 × 27 in. (104 × 69 cm)
Courtesy of the Tony Nourmand Collection

**Girls On The Loose** (1958)
US 41 × 27 in. (104 × 69 cm)
Courtesy of the Tony Nourmand Collection

Many B-movies were directed by ex-Hollywood men who shifted to low-budget projects out of financial necessity. *Girls On The Loose* was directed by Paul Henreid; better known as the actor who played Ingrid Bergman's husband in *Casablanca*. Similarly, *Reform School Girl* was written and directed by Edward Bernds; a former Columbia Pictures director famous for his comedy work with the Three Stooges.

**Reform School Girl** (1957)
US 41 × 27 in. (104 × 69 cm)
Courtesy of the Tony Nourmand Collection

**Girl Gang** (1954)
US 54 × 41 in. (137 × 104 cm)
Courtesy of the Tony Nourmand Collection

Having been immersed in the industry since birth, **Dan Sonney** (1915–2002) became an exploitation giant. His father was Louis Sonney, who had toured with Dwain Esper on films such as *Sex Maniac* (1934). Dan started producing his own films as soon as he was able and used all the same tricks of the trade that his father had taught him, as the sensationalist and 'shocking' poster for *The Wild And Wicked* demonstrates. In the early 60s, Sonney joined forces with David F. Friedman and together they formed an impressive and successful partnership, presiding over a colossal exploitation market in the 60s and early 70s.

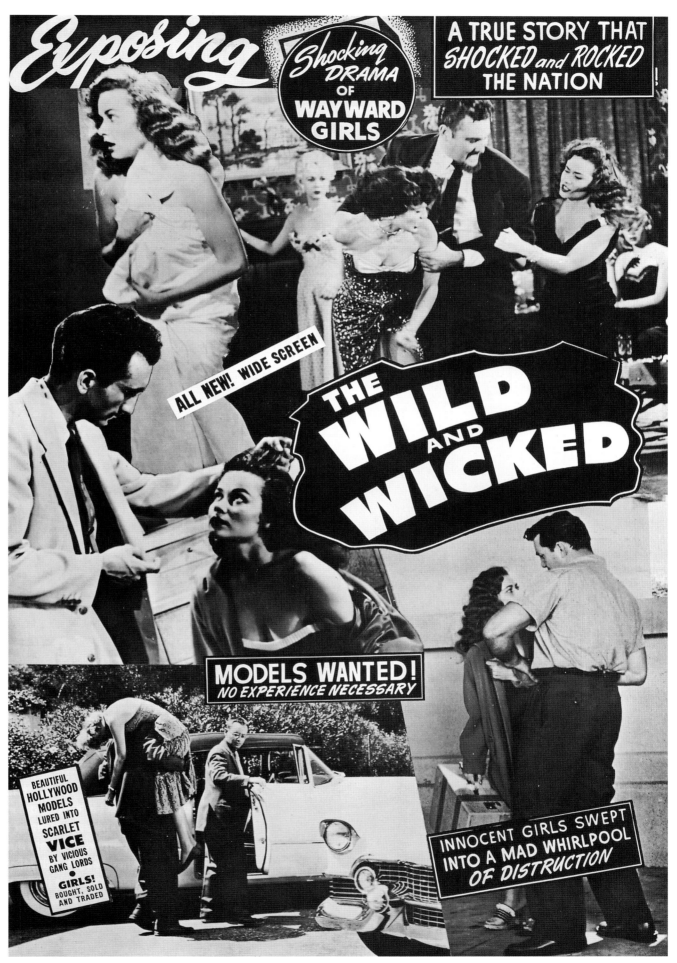

**The Flesh Merchant (The Wild And Wicked)** (1956)
US 41 × 27 in. (104 × 69 cm)
Courtesy of the Tony Nourmand Collection

**She Shoulda Said No (The Devil's Weed / Wild Weed)** (1949)
British 30 × 40 in. (76 × 102 cm)
Courtesy of the Tony Nourmand Collection

Starring Lila Leeds, *She Shoulda Said No* (also known as *The Devil's Weed*) is based on the real-life drug bust the actress experienced with Robert Mitchum. The misdemeanour resulted in Leeds spending time in prison and MGM hastily ending her contract. Her career seemed to be finished for good until exploitation mogul Kroger Babb hired her for *The Devil's Weed*. Whilst touring with the film, Leeds did nothing (or perhaps everything) to enhance her reputation, engaging in lascivious behaviour and being arrested in further drug raids. For added authenticity, Leeds purportedly wore the same clothes on camera as she had worn when caught with Mitchum. It was this reality pitch that helped turn the movie into an instant success.

In 1956 the film was banned in Pennsylvania. However, the verdict was, remarkably, overturned after a court ruled that the original decision had been unconstitutional. This was a massive coup for the exploitation industry.

**She Shoulda Said No (The Devil's Weed / Wild Weed)** (1949)
US 41 × 27 in. (104 × 69 cm)
Courtesy of the Tony Nourmand Collection

**Sex Madness (Human Wreckage)** (1938)
US 42 × 28 in. (107 × 71 cm)
Courtesy of the Tony Nourmand Collection

A veteran of World War I, **Dwain Esper** (1892–1982) was christened 'King of the Celluloid Gypsies', a fitting title for the most infamous of the 'Forty Thieves'. A shrewd salesman, Esper marketed his films as 'educational', thus giving his audiences the opportunity to persuade themselves that rather than enjoying his steamy, titillating movies, they were widening their knowledge of important social issues. Esper was braver than many of his contemporaries and showed nudity and explicit drug-taking when no one else would. His golden age was the 30s and some of his better-known titles include *Human Wreckage*, *Narcotic*, *Assassin Of Youth* and *Marihuana: Weed With Roots In Hell*. *Narcotic* showed an endless spectrum of drugs and injecting methods and was shocking, even for the exploitation industry, in its detailed depictions. For good measure, it also featured lots of sex and prostitution. It was while on the road with *Narcotic* that Esper boosted ticket sales by displaying the corpse of 'Elmer The Dope Fiend'. The preserved cadaver was, in fact, that of a former highway-man that Esper had acquired from a circus on the cheap.

**Narcotic** (1933)
US 81 × 41 in. (206 × 104 cm)
Courtesy of the Chris Dark Collection

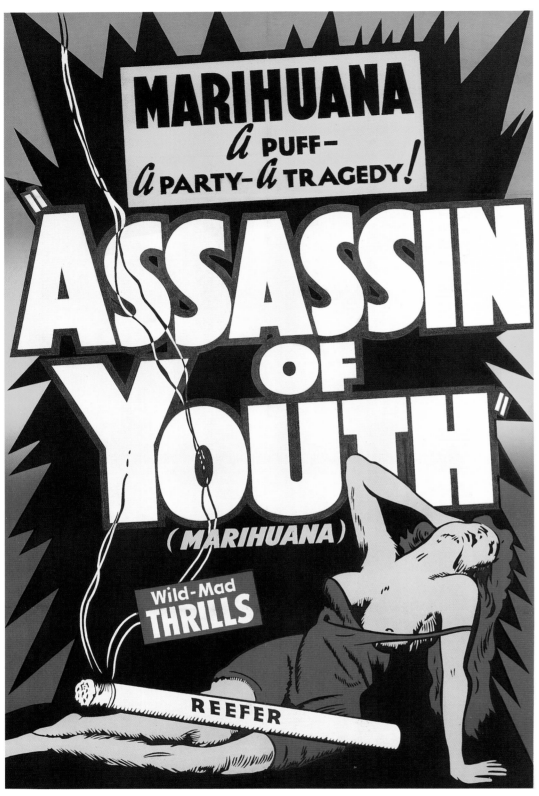

**Assassin Of Youth** (1937)
US 41 × 27 in. (104 × 69 cm)
Courtesy of the Martin Bridgewater Collection

In 1932, the Federal Bureau of Narcotics was established under the direction of Harry J. Anslinger. He proceeded to stir the public into an anti-marijuana frenzy, perpetuating the myth that users of the drug had embarked upon an irreversible descent into an underworld of crime and loose living. In his lectures Anslinger explained that marijuana use was the root cause of crime and unemployment in poor areas; for good measure, he also blamed the immigrant and working-class population for introducing the drug into these neighbourhoods. No evidence was produced to support such claims, yet this did not stop Anslinger's ideas from attaining the status of revealed truth. In the mid-30s, the *American Journal of Medicine* pronounced that 'Marijuana users … will kill or maim without reason'. The only significant challenge to such wild statements was made by the mayor of New York, who ordered an independent and impartial investigation into the effects of the 'weed with roots in hell'. When it became clear that the investigators had concluded that marijuana had none of the alleged mind-altering and crime-causing effects, Anslinger quickly destroyed all known copies of their report, preventing its publication.

Exploitation has always been quick to seize upon contemporary scandals and scare stories, and the 30s saw a massive upsurge of films dealing with the 'tragedy' of marijuana. *Marihuana: Weed With Roots In Hell* and *Assassin Of Youth* are two perfect examples of the sensationalist and absurd propaganda ostensibly intended to stop people using the drug. The title of the latter was actually borrowed from an article written by Anslinger himself.

**Marihuana: Weed With Roots In Hell** (1935)
US 41 × 27 in. (104 × 69 cm)
Courtesy of the Tony Nourmand Collection

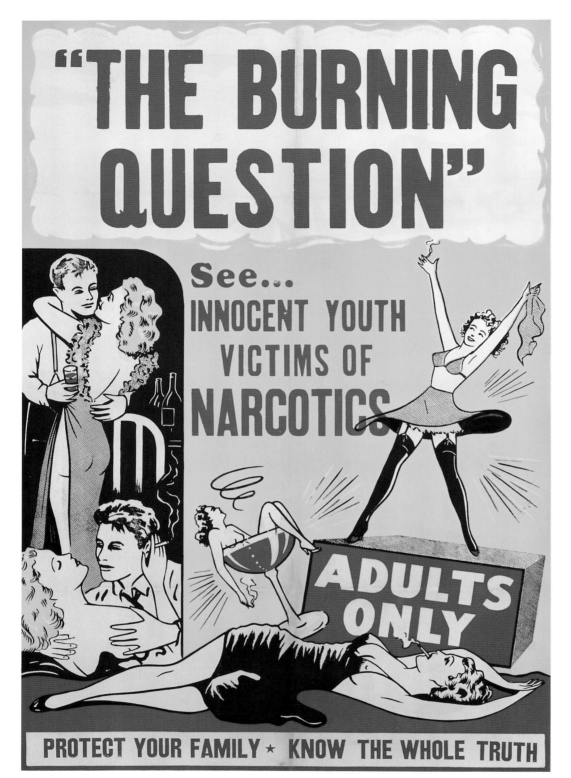

**Tell Your Children (The Burning Question / Reefer Madness)** (1936)
US 41 × 27 in. (104 × 69 cm)
(Style A)
Courtesy of the Tony Nourmand Collection

*The Burning Question* was made by a Los Angeles church group in an attempt to lure the young away from a drug-fuelled life of sin and debauchery. Ironically, it has become one of the biggest cult films ever made.

● **1894.** *Opium Joint*, the first US film dealing with drugs, is made.
● **1909.** The Opium Exclusion Act is passed, banning the importation and use of opium.
● **1914.** The Harrison Narcotics Act is passed.
● **1919.** The Volstead Act is passed, outlawing drugs and alcohol; this is the beginning of Prohibition.
● **1931.** All but two US States outlaw marijuana.
● **1932.** The Federal Bureau of Narcotics is created.

**Tell Your Children (The Burning Question / Reefer Madness)** (1936)
US 41 × 27 in. (104 × 69 cm)
(Style B)
Courtesy of the Tony Nourmand Collection

**The Pace That Kills** (1936)
US 22 × 14 in. (56 × 36 cm)
Courtesy of the Tony Nourmand Collection

*The Pace That Kills* tells the story of a good, honest country boy who moves to the city and quickly succumbs to the temptations of vice and depravity. His life spirals out of control and by the end of the film, he and his girlfriend have both committed suicide. This classic exploitation tale tapped right into one of the central issues of 20s America.

The Progressive movement was borne out of the devastating depression of the 1890s and it sought to cure a number of social ills. Although its aims were theoretically idealistic, in reality progressivism often bred prejudice and racism. The countryside was perceived as a golden utopia, in contrast to the sinful city. The working class and immigrants were blamed for undermining American society and threatening the achievement of the noble aims of 'greater democracy and social justice' – the benefits that would accrue from the achievement of these aspirations were, perhaps not unexpectedly, reserved for the white middle classes. The movement enjoyed a resurgence in the 'Jazz Age' of the 20s when cities were experiencing a cultural revolution, with fashion, music, intellectual life and moral life all being transformed by new ideas. Tales of 'flapper girls' and 'jazz men' and the work of writers like T. S. Elliot and F. Scott Fitzgerald filtered back to rural America where they were seen as symptoms of metropolitan decadence, a view which movies like *The Pace That Kills* confirmed and exploited to the hilt.

**Cocaine (The Thrill That Kills)** (c.1940s)
US 41 × 27 in. (104 × 69 cm)

**Devil's Harvest** (1942)
US 42 × 28 in. (106 × 71 cm)
(Style B)
Courtesy of the Martin Bridgewater Collection

The 40s saw a decline in films about marijuana. With America now at war, the focus was firmly on portraying Americans as happy warriors engaged in a noble mission – no one wanted to dwell on domestic problems such as drug use. There was also a practical issue, as Japanese sources of rope began to dwindle, growing domestic hemp became a patriotic activity; especially after 1942 when the US government introduced its 'Hemp For Victory' campaign, releasing films that showed farmers wading through fields of hemp. Such footage naturally took the edge off the marijuana paranoia.

The exploitation industry, however, was reluctant to abandon a theme that had proved so profitable and *Devil's Harvest* gave the marijuana flick a new and topical twist by attributing America's drug problems to the Nazis.

**Devil's Harvest** (1942)
US 41 × 27 in. (104 × 69 cm)

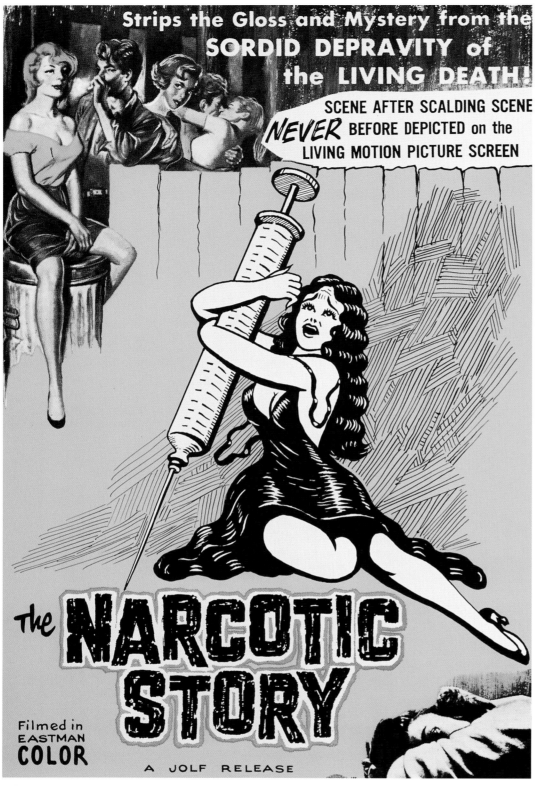

**The Narcotic Story** (1958)
US 41 × 27 in. (104 × 69 cm)
Courtesy of the Tony Nourmand Collection

Heroin was first discovered in 1898 by a German scientist who patented it as a cough suppressant. The drug was not suspected of being addictive for a long time and was even used as a cure for morphine addiction. By the 50s, however, the dangers of heroin had become apparent and *The Narcotic Story* and *One-Way Ticket To Hell* exploited the opportunities offered by this new menace. The latter was, in fact, pretty undiscriminating, warning against a whole host of social menaces, including marijuana, heroin, teenagers, motorbikes and 'nasty foreigners'. (The film was so low-budget that the producer's parents were in the cast.) Both films were part of a dying cycle of 'myth and menace' exploitation drug films that inevitably faded away in the face of Hollywood's increasingly honest depiction of the issue.

In 1956, Otto Preminger released *The Man With The Golden Arm*. Influenced by Italian neo-realism, it dealt with drug addiction in an open and realistic way, avoiding all the sensationalist traps of the past. Having been refused a seal by the Breen Office, Preminger went ahead and released the film with his own funds. This was a major coup for mainstream cinema and exerted massive pressure on the Production Code Office to rewrite the Hays Code. In the very same year, the Code was amended to permit the portrayal of drug addiction, prostitution and childbirth so long as they were presented in good taste. This was the beginning of the end; twelve years later, the infamous Hays Code was finally abandoned altogether.

**Teenage Devil Dolls (One-Way Ticket To Hell)** (1952)
US 41 × 27 in. (104 × 69 cm)
Courtesy of the Tony Nourmand Collection

**Big Jim McLain (Marijuana)** (1952)
Italian 79 × 55 in. (201 × 140 cm)
Art by Luigi Martinati
Courtesy of the Tony Nourmand Collection

The original version of *Big Jim McLain* is set during the hysterical Red scare of the McCarthy years and follows the exploits of an American government operative who is sent to Hawaii to root out a communist cell. Marijuana plays no part whatsoever in the original story, but the film's Italian distributors felt that its plot had little relevance to audiences there, so when the film was dubbed the dialogue was adapted so that John Wayne's government agent appears to be cracking down on the illegal drug trade rather than undercover communists. It was this aspect of the film that Luigi Martinati chose to depict in the Italian poster campaign.

**Luigi Martinati** (1893–1984) had a prolific career in film poster art. Born in Florence, he moved to Rome in 1911 and started as an artist's apprentice. He became the manager of one of the leading advertising agencies in Rome, where he worked for a number of film companies, notably Warner Brothers. In the mid-40s, he joined forces with two other giants of Italian film poster design, Anselmo Ballester and Alfredo Capitani, to form a company devoted exclusively to the production of film posters. Between them, the three artists produced an endless stream of striking, memorable images. Martinati's personal style is characterized by a large portrait shot combined with a smaller scene in the foreground. This is illustrated on both posters for *Big Jim McLain*.

**Big Jim McLain (Marijuana)** (1952)
Italian 55 × 39 in. (140 × 99 cm)
Art by Luigi Martinati
Courtesy of the Martin Bridgewater Collection

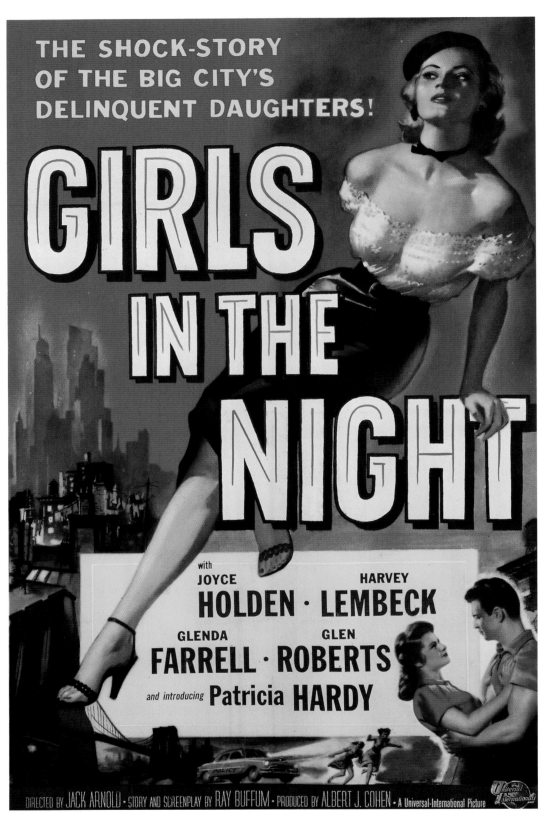

**Girls In The Night** (1953)
US 41 × 27 in. (104 × 69 cm)
Art by Reynold Brown
Courtesy of the Tony Nourmand Collection

*The Respectful Prostitute* was based on a play of the same name by Jean-Paul Sartre. First published in 1946, it was a damning critique of racism in the deep south of the United States. In America, the film, which followed six years later, was treated as a simple exploitation flick – promoted with the usual plethora of sensationalist advertising imagery and taglines. In France, however, the approach was quite the opposite. **Roger Rojac's** (1913–1997) artwork for the French poster managed to soberly convey the underlying tension of the film. And by replacing the word *Putain* – the French for prostitute – with a discreet 'P... ', the lettering de-emphasized the theme of prostitution.

**La Putain Respectueuse (The Respectful Prostitute)** (1952)
French 63 × 47 in. (160 × 119 cm)
Art by Roger Rojac
Courtesy of the Tony Nourmand Collection

**Escort Girl** (1941)
US 41 × 27 in. (104 × 69 cm)
Courtesy of the Liza Tesei Collection

*Girl Of The Night* was released in America in 1960. Although suggestive, the title was still fairly coy and avoided stating outright that this was a story about prostitution. When the film was released in a more liberal Sweden, however, there were no such concerns and the *Call Girl* title left absolutely no ambiguity as to the subject matter.

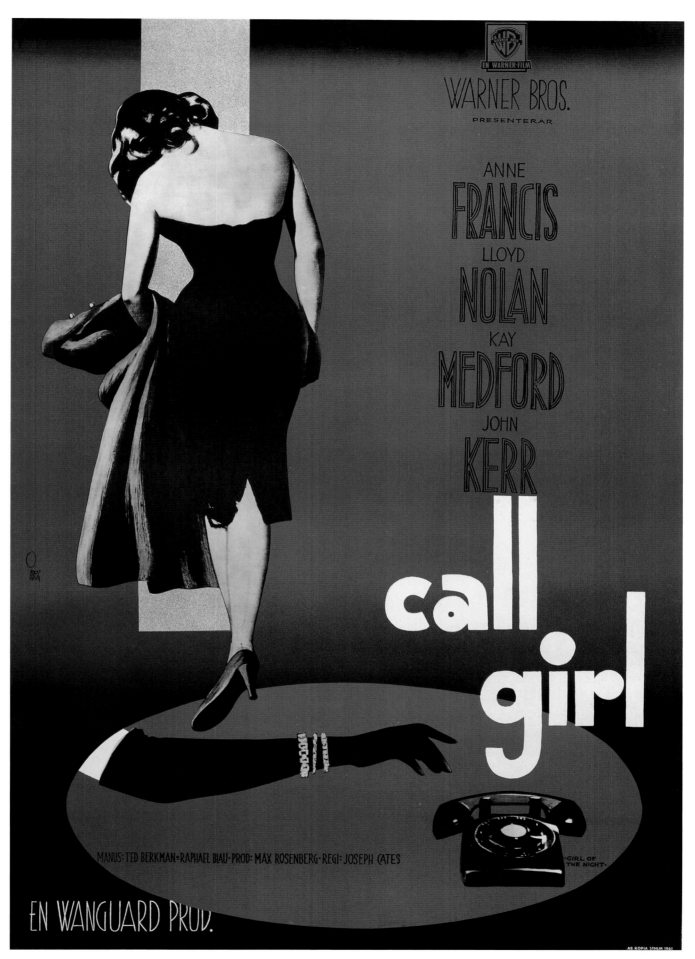

**Girl Of The Night (Call Girl)** (1960)
Swedish 39 × 27 in. (99 × 69 cm)
Art by Gosta Aberg
Courtesy of the Tony Nourmand Collection

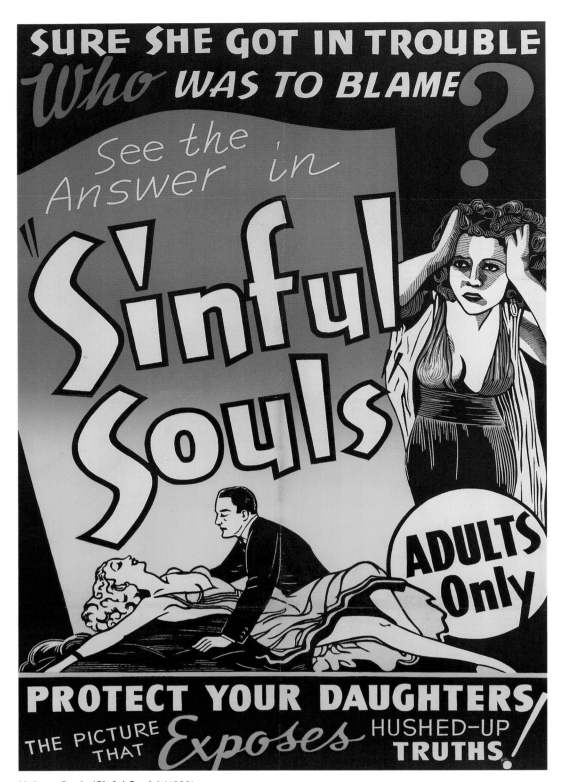

**Unborn Souls (Sinful Souls)** (1939)
US 41 × 28 in. (104 × 71 cm)
Courtesy of the Tony Nourmand Collection

Originally released with the title *Unborn Souls*, *Sinful Souls* dealt with the taboo subjects of birth control and abortion. The film was renamed in order to appeal to a wider audience.

*Sinful Souls*, along with *Main Street Girls*, used the classic exploitation technique of presenting sensational subject matter under the guise of education. Both films claimed to 'expose' parents to the evils that lurked ready to seduce and corrupt their innocent daughters.

- **1873.** The Comstock Law is passed, outlawing the importation, production, sale or use of contraceptives. The law also disallowed any educational or written reference to birth control.
- **1916.** Margaret Sanger opens the first public clinic for counselling on contraception and birth control.
- **1923.** The first physician-staffed birth control clinic opens in the US.
- **1937.** Contraception has become a $250 million business.

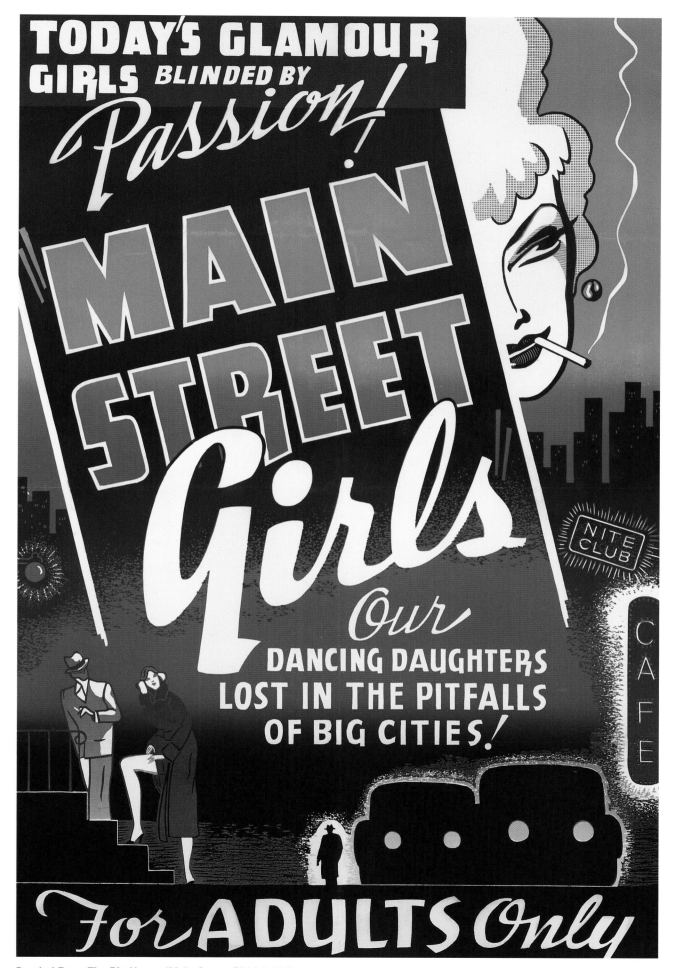

**Paroled From The Big House (Main Street Girls)** (1936)
US 41 × 27 in. (104 × 69 cm)
Courtesy of the Tony Nourmand Collection

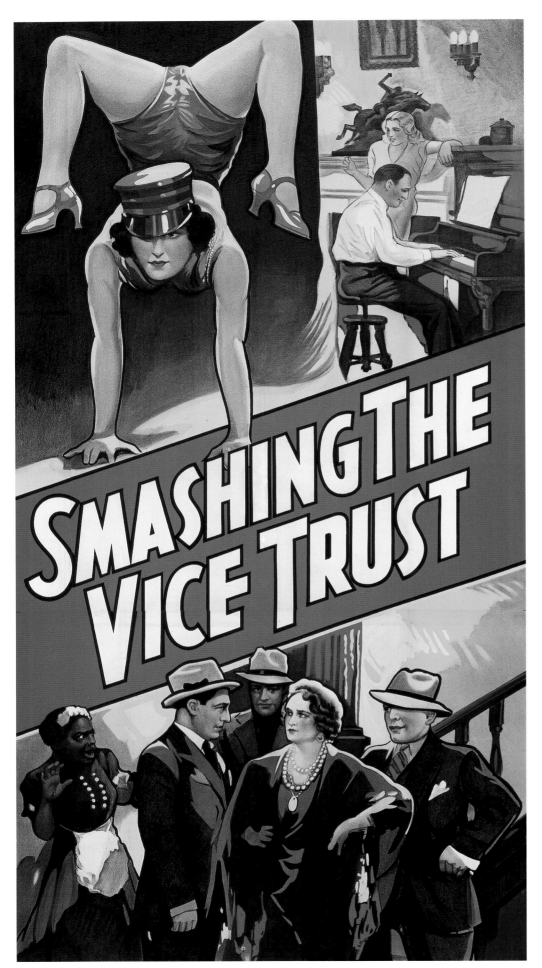

**Smashing The Vice Trust** (1937)
US 81 × 41 in. (206 × 104 cm)
Courtesy of the Tony Nourmand Collection

*Smashing The Vice Trust* and *The Wages Of Sin* dealt with prostitution, gambling and white slavery. Both films were loosely based on the character of 'Lucky' Luciano – a major New York gangster who was arrested in the early 30s on prostitution charges. The case dominated the headlines for months and encouraged a public awareness and fear of vice rings. The fact that Luciano was a dark-skinned Italian also served to reinforce the prevalent racist belief that foreigners and immigrants were to blame for social degeneration. *The Wages Of Sin* took advantage of the public interest in the Luciano case by flashing the following message to audiences at the end of the film: 'The jury is still out. What will the verdict be? What would your verdict be? $100.00 in cash prizes will be given for the best answer – contest open to all.'

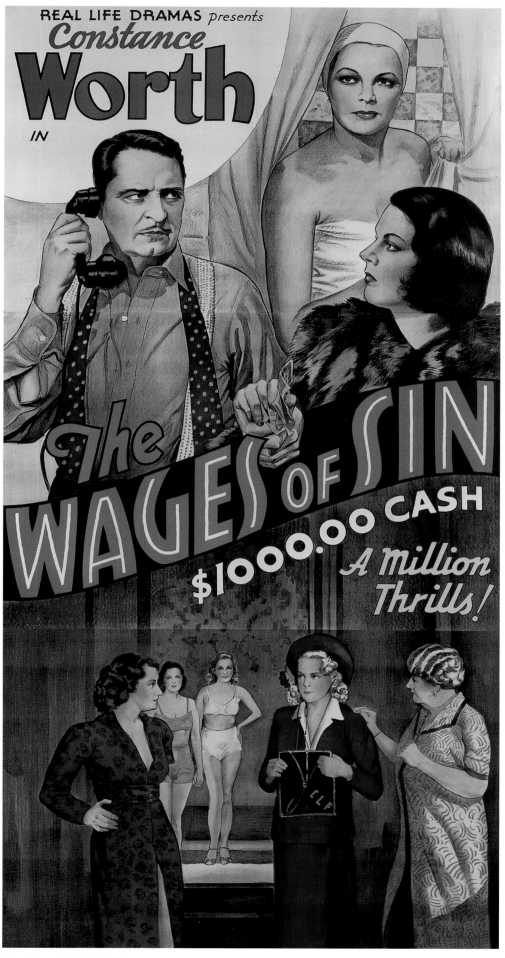

**The Wages Of Sin** (1938)
US 81 × 41 in. (206 × 104 cm)
Courtesy of the Tony Nourmand Collection

**Gambling With Souls (The Vice Racket)** (1936)
US 25 × 22 in. (64 × 56 cm)
Courtesy of the Tony Nourmand Collection

*Gambling With Souls* was another film based on 'Lucky' and was released in the same year that Luciano came to trial. After failing to secure a theatrical release under its original title, it was re-released the following year as *The Vice Racket*. The film was advertised in a number of different guises, as many exploitation titles were. The US poster for *Gambling With Souls* suggests a light and romantic, if mildly titillating, flick. In contrast, the poster for *The Vice Racket* is much more hard-hitting and sensationalist.

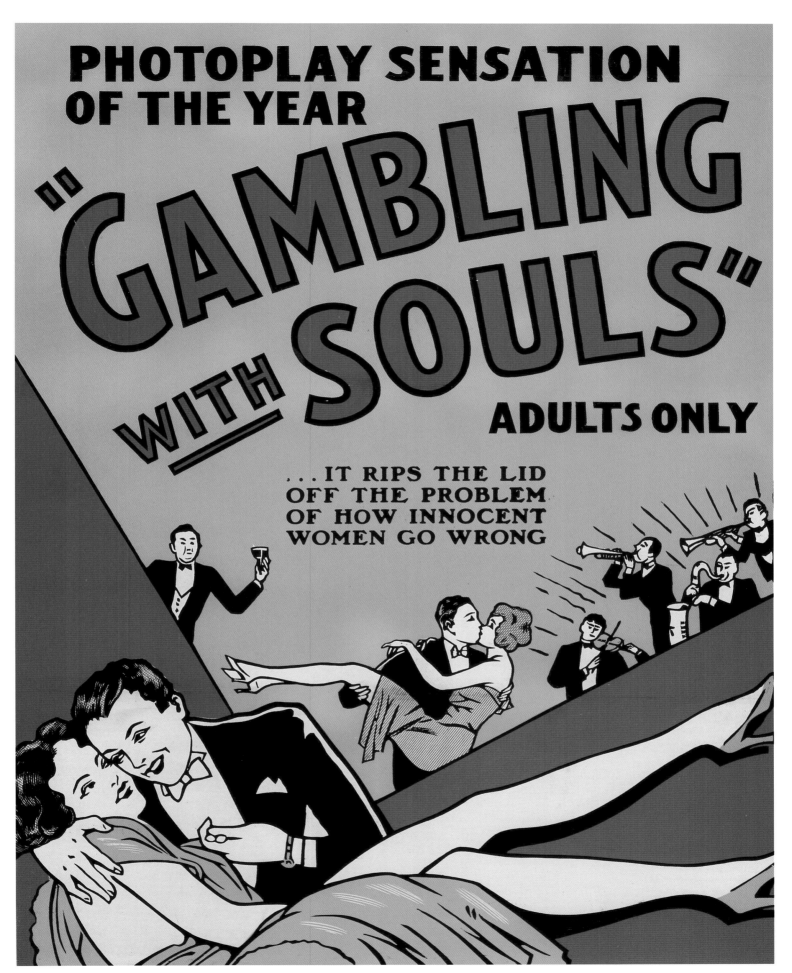

**Gambling With Souls (The Vice Racket)** (1936)
US 41 × 27 in. (104 × 69 cm)
Courtesy of the Tony Nourmand Collection

**Gambling With Souls (The Vice Racket)** (1936)
US 60 × 40 in. (152 × 102 cm)
(Board Display)
Courtesy of the Tony Nourmand Collection

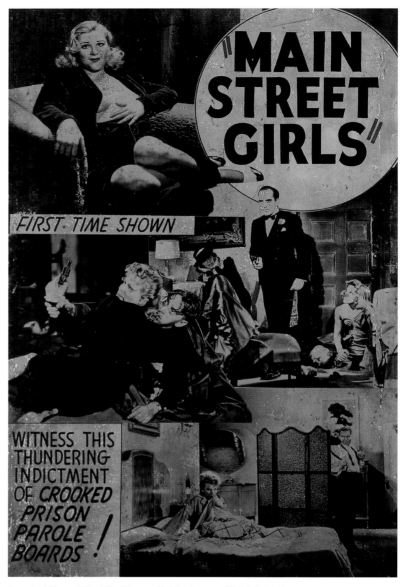

**Paroled From The Big House (Main Street Girls)** (1936)
US 60 × 40 in. (152 × 102 cm)
(Board Display)
Courtesy of the Tony Nourmand Collection

Exploitation producers were masters of advertising and all stops were pulled out to promote a film. The theatre lobby was usually the place to start and it would be covered inside and out with an assortment of posters, gimmicks, pamphlets and props. A collage of photographs, stills and taglines would be pasted on to large display boards that were then coated with varnish. Cheap and eye-catching, the display boards were intended to persuade audiences that they offered a mere preview of the titillating delights that awaited them within.

**Gambling With Souls (The Vice Racket)** (1936)
US 60 × 40 in. (152 × 102 cm)
(Board Display)
Courtesy of the Tony Nourmand Collection

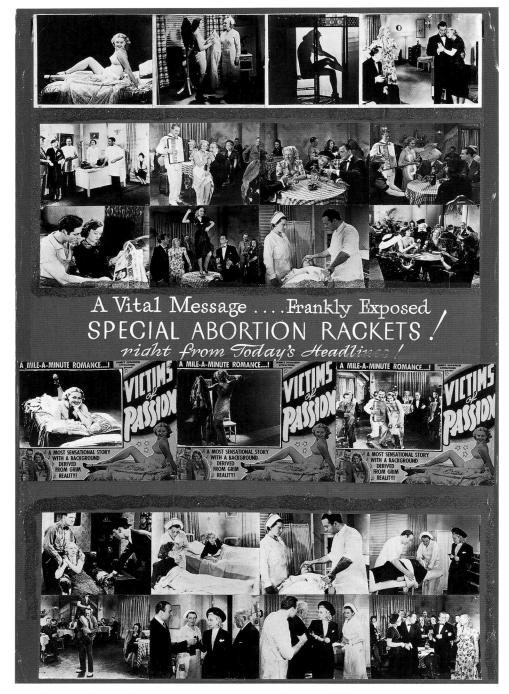

**Race Suicide (Victims Of Passion / Special Abortion Rackets)** (1937)
US 60 × 40 in. (152 × 102 cm)
(Board Display)
Courtesy of the Tony Nourmand Collection

● 'The chief of blessings for any nation is that it shall leave its seed to inherit the land. The greatest of all curses is sterility, and the severest of all condemnations should be visited upon wilful sterility.'
(US President Theodore Roosevelt.)
● 'For a case like this I can find no words so apt as "race suicide". There is no bloodshed, no violence, no assault of the race that waxes upon the race that wanes. The higher race quietly and unmurmuringly eliminates itself.'
(Dr. Edward Ross discussing the implications of the decline in Caucasian birth-rates in his 1901 article *The Causes Of Racial Superiority*.)

As President of the United States from 1901 to 1909, Theodore Roosevelt believed that many of the problems in American society were ultimately rooted in the decline of birth-rates among the middle and upper classes. He favoured the phrase 'race suicide' and defined it as the wilful decision to have a small family or practise birth control by means of illegal abortions. Although Roosevelt was a populist he shared the widespread assumption, promoted by the Eugenics movement, that it was the duty of white Anglo-Saxons to procreate and maintain the 'purity' of the ruling classes. It was widely believed at this time that the immigrant and working-class population was increasing exponentially and was in danger of 'polluting' established society.

The Eugenics movement began on the East Coast of America in the early twentieth century and was founded on contemporary genetic theories and the social Darwinism that was in fashion at this time. The Eugenicists believed that breeding should be controlled so that the more 'advanced' white races continued to pre-dominate. They supported Roosevelt's push for larger white families, and also sought to discourage procreation amongst the 'lower' races. They did this by lobbying for restrictions on immigration and encouraging the sterilization of the mentally and physically handicapped (and any other sectors of society deemed 'unfit.')

In the early 30s, two of exploitation's most successful roadshow men, Dwain Esper and Louis Sonney, decided to take a film called *Maniac* on the road. The film, which was about a crazed scientist, was a flop until they cunningly renamed it *Sex Maniac*. The crowds then began lining up around the block.

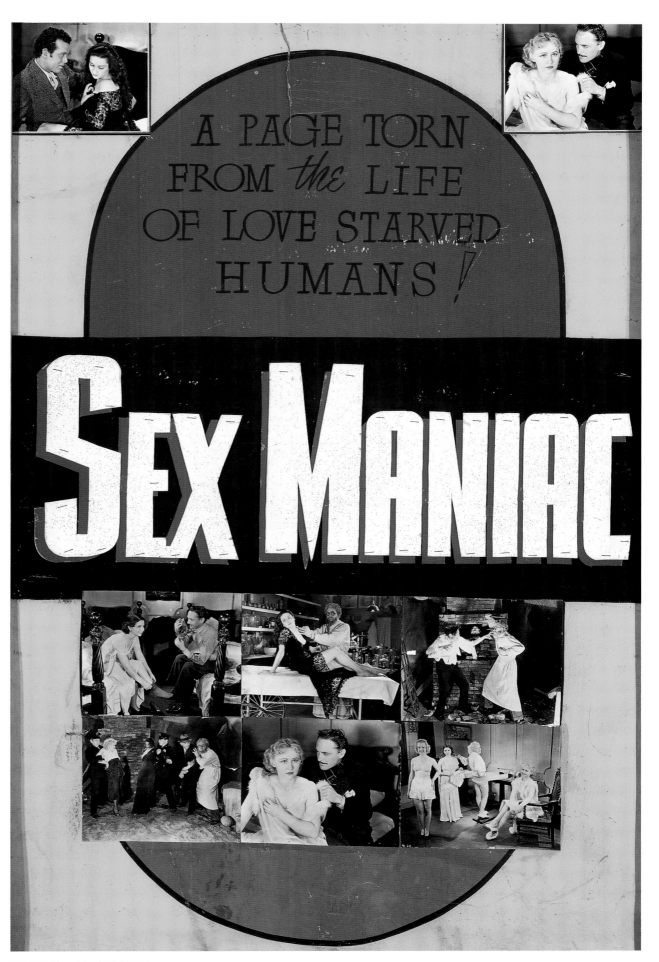

**Maniac (Sex Maniac)** (1934)
US 60 × 40 in. (152 × 102 cm)
(Board Display)
Courtesy of the Tony Nourmand Collection

**Slaves In Bondage** (1937)
US 41 × 27 in. (104 × 69 cm)
(Style B)
Courtesy of the Richard Loncraine Collection

The two posters for *Slaves In Bondage* reveal ways in which the exploitation industry adopted a variety of different promotional approaches depending on the circumstances. When the film was given a heavily censored theatrical release, thought and money were poured into the advertising campaign; the result being a colourful stone lithograph. But when the less censored version of the same film was taken on the roadshow circuit, the poster was printed coarsely with minimal use of colour – a prime example of cheap, sensationalist roadshow art.

**Slaves In Bondage** (1937)
US 41 × 27 in. (104 × 69 cm)
(Style A)
Courtesy of the Tony Nourmand Collection

**Mom And Dad** (1945)
US 41 × 27 in. (104 × 69 cm)

*Mom And Dad* was the most successful classic exploitation film ever made. It played for 23 years, was involved in over 400 court proceedings and grossed over $100 million. The genius behind this *tour de force* was **Kroger Babb** (1906–1980). With a carnival background, Babb was a natural huckster and he used every trick available with *Mom And Dad*. He called his production company Hygienic Productions and, in keeping with traditional exploitation flick practice, he portrayed the film as morally worthy. Men and women were given separate screenings and the film opened with a request for the audience to stand and sing the Star Spangled Banner. Both gimmicks helped emphasize the 'honourable', all-American intentions of the film. Halfway through the movie there was an interval during which the audience was addressed by Elliot Forbes, a 'professor' of sex hygiene, who gave a lecture on the importance of the young knowing the facts of life. Forbes then offered the audience the chance to buy a book, *The Secrets Of Sensible Sex*, which usually raked in a few extra dollars for Babb.

The success of *Mom And Dad* was not only a result of Babb's 'hard sell' strategy; the content of the film itself was another determining factor. It follows the story of a young girl who ends up pregnant through her ignorance of the facts of life. So far, this was no different to the traditional exploitation formula. What made *Mom And Dad* different were the three extra reels added to the film. These showed gory close-ups of victims of venereal disease, a caesarean birth and, the *pièce de résistance*, an actual live birth, filmed in close-up. Audiences loved it and Babb used the usual trick to avoid the attention of local censors; if the film was being shown in a state or city where censorship was particularly strict, he would simply remove the 'hot' reels and screen a 'cold' version of the film, minus the extras.

*Mom And Dad* proved influential and several makers of exploitation films began copying Babb's tactics, as the poster for *Because Of Eve* illustrates. More significantly, however, Babb had caught Hollywood's attention and in 1948 Universal Studios used the *Mom And Dad* template to make *The Story Of Bob And Alice*. Ironically, the film was banned under the Hays Code and was therefore sold on to the exploitation circuit.

You'll Gasp—
You'll Wince—
You'll Shudder—

BUT YOU WON'T TAKE YOUR EYES OFF THE SCREEN

# BECAUSE of EVE "THE STORY OF LIFE"

A Tender, Vital Story Of A Man And Wife Who Were Ignorant Of The Facts Of Life!

## ADULTS ONLY
WOMEN ONLY AND HIGH SCHOOL AGE GIRLS ▪ 2 AND 7 P. M.

MEN ONLY AND HIGH SCHOOL AGE BOYS ▪ 9:00 P. M.

Recommended by PARENTS, CLERGY, TEACHERS !

EXTRA - ON STAGE - IN PERSON
THE EMINENT HYGIENE COMMENTATOR
MR. ALEXANDER LEEDS

**Because Of Eve** (1948)
US 60 × 40 in. (152 × 102 cm)
Courtesy of the Tony Nourmand Collection

**Mondo Cane** (1961)
US 41 × 27 in. (104 × 69 cm)
Courtesy of the Tony Nourmand Collection

The *Mondo Cane* series of films is racist, violent and shocking, with few, if any, redeeming features. Yet, as is the case with many exploitation titles, they remain interesting period pieces that give us a valuable insight into the standards and morals of yesteryear. The *Mondo Cane* series was also significant in creating the 'voyeur' cinematic genre and spawned an endless stream of imitators. A huge hit at drive-ins, the series remained popular throughout the 60s.

The American and Polish *Mondo Cane* posters cast interesting light on the differing ways in which the film was perceived and promoted in the two countries. While the American approach was to use the poster to highlight the nudity and the 'documentary' aspects of the film, the Polish rendition gives nothing away. Striking in its simplicity, the design by **Wojciech Zamecznik** (1923–1967) combines photography with sleek graphic elements – a fitting example of the artist's unique style.

**Mondo Cane (Pieski Swiat)** (1961)
Polish 33 × 23 in. (84 × 58 cm)
Art by Wojciech Zamecznik
Courtesy of the Tony Nourmand Collection

**Women In The Night (Curse Of A Teenage Nazi)** (1948)
US 41 × 27 in. (104 × 69 cm)
Courtesy of the Horst Keller Collection

The Second World War was still raging when the exploitation industry started churning out films about the evils of National Socialism. The 40s are littered with movies that followed the usual formula, but replaced the drug or vice menace with a Nazi theme. The 60s and 70s, on the other hand, saw a much more perverse form of exploitation in which Nazism was used as a pretext for depicting extreme violence and sadomasochism. Operating on the midnight drive-in circuit, the most famous of this cycle of films was *Ilsa: She Wolf Of The SS*, which remains an underground cult classic.

The film is based on the real-life character of Ilse Koch who was infamous for her violent abuse of prisoners at Buchenwald concentration camp. She was also renowned for her sexuality and brutality. These elements are combined in *She Wolf Of The SS*. The poster tagline 'I turned my lovers into lampshades!' was also based on Koch. When she was arrested at the end of the war, furniture was found in her apartment that was apparently made of human skin. (Although it was later proved to be made of goatskin, the legend had been born.) Ilse Koch was executed after the International War Crime Tribunal found her guilty of crimes against humanity. The character would, however, return in numerous sequels throughout the 70s.

Ilsa, She Wolf Of The SS (1975)
US 41 × 27 in. (104 × 69 cm)
Courtesy of the Horst Keller Collection

**The Black Klansman (I Crossed The Color Line / I Crossed The Line)** (1966)
US 41 × 27 in. (104 × 69 cm)
(Style A)

*The Black Gestapo* was a run-of-the-mill blaxploitation film that featured extreme violence. It was unusual, however, in that it featured black-on-black violence and the ultimate 'villain' of the piece was the gang itself which is corrupted by power. The film was originally released under the less provocative title, *Ghetto Warriors*.

**Ghetto Warriors (The Black Gestapo)** (1975)
US 41 × 27 in. (104 × 69 cm)
(Withdrawn)
Art by Ken Barr

**I Passed For White** (1960)
US 41 × 27 in. (104 × 69 cm)

The Civil Rights Movement was the defining issue of American domestic politics in the 60s and exploitation filmmakers were ready, as ever, to capitalize on a debate that led to social tension and confusion. With titles like *I Passed For White* and *I Crossed The Color Line* (also known as *The Black Klansman*) exploitation found new themes that would appeal to contemporary audiences.

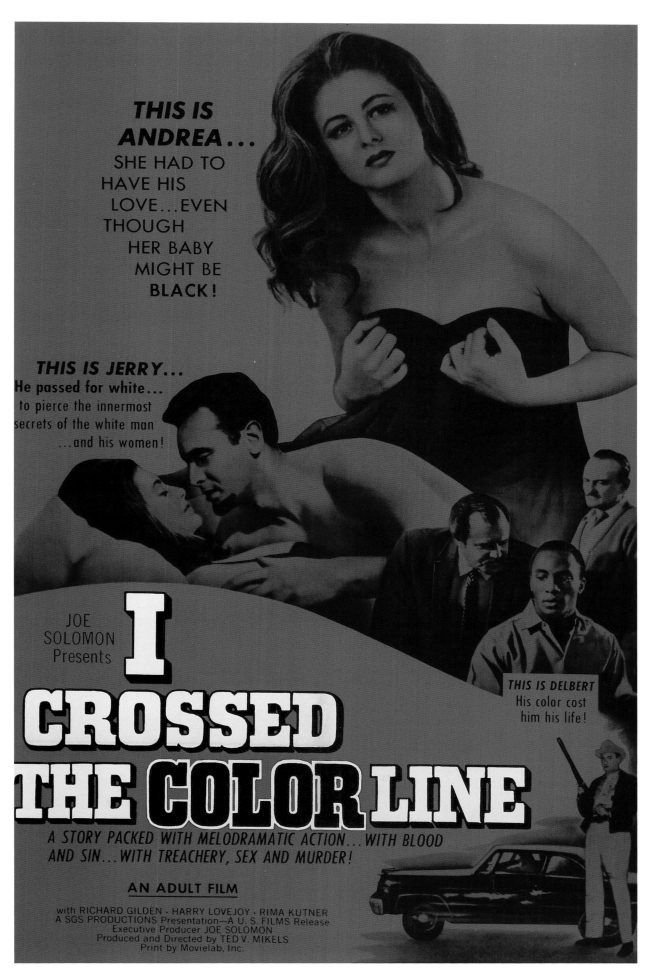

**The Black Klansman (I Crossed The Color Line / I Crossed The Line)** (1966)
US 41 × 27 in. (104 × 69cm)
(Style B)

A film of
MELVIN VAN PEEBLES

YOU BLED MY MOMMA — YOU BLED MY POPPA — BUT YOU WONT BLEED ME

ORIGINAL SOUNDTRACK ALBUM AVAILABLE ON STAX RECORDS    ORIGINAL PAPERBACK SOON AVAILABLE AS A LANCER PUBLICATION
MELVIN VAN PEEBLES and JERRY GROSS present "SWEET SWEETBACK'S BAADASSSSS SONG"
a CINEMATION INDUSTRIES Release · COLOR

RATED
BY AN
ALL-WHITE JURY

**Sweet Sweetback's Baad Asssss Song** (1971)
US 41 × 27 in. (104 × 69 cm)
Courtesy of the Tony Nourmand Collection

Civil unrest was rife in the 70s and, despite the legal triumphs of the Civil Rights Movement in the 60s, black Americans still faced racism in all aspects of their daily lives. It was against this backdrop that independent filmmaker Melvin Van Peebles decided to reclaim some power and took it upon himself to write, direct and star in *Sweet Sweetback's Baad Asssss Song*. With its righteous anger against white, reactionary society, *Sweetback* was infused with the spirit of the Black Power movement. The highest grossing independent film of its day, Van Peebles' creation was an instant hit. For the first time, a film achieved success on the back of black box-office returns alone and, at a time when five out of every six Hollywood 'blockbusters' were failing, mainstream studios rapidly sat up and took notice.

MGM were the first to respond, releasing *Shaft* within a year of *Sweetback*.  It turned out to be a very adroit move, for the film not only became a massive nationwide success, but also initiated the whole new genre that would quickly become known as 'blaxploitation'. *Shaft* firmly established the formula for the genre: a powerful, attractive, black protagonist fights with attitude and charisma against 'the man' while enjoying the admiration of several beautiful women. The hero was always cool, ruthless and fashionable and strode through the action accompanied by a soundtrack of smooth, catchy music – a popular trademark of many blaxploitation titles. Written by Isaac Hayes, *Shaft's* theme song became a huge radio hit. Its legendary soundtrack won an Oscar and a Grammy and went Platinum.

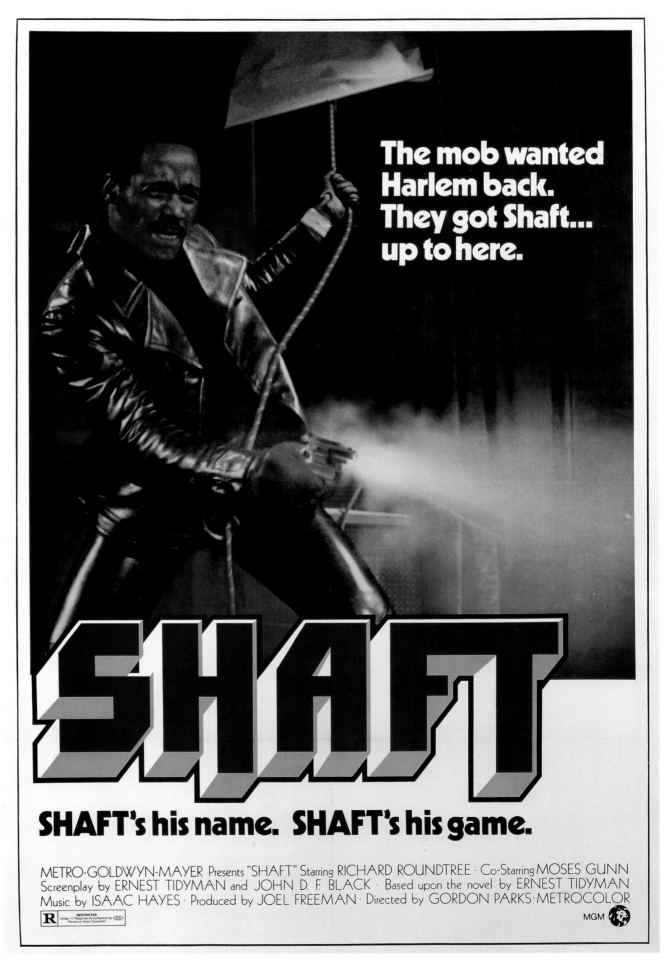

**Shaft** (1971)
US 41 × 27 in. (104 × 69 cm)
Courtesy of the Tony Nourmand Collection

**Never a dude like this one!
He's got a plan to stick it to The Man!**

THE
SIG SHORE
PRODUCTION

**Super Fly**

See
and hear
CURTIS
MAYFIELD
play his
Super Fly
score!

Original soundtrack available on Curtom Records

The SIG SHORE Production "SUPER FLY" Starring RON O'NEAL · CARL LEE · JULIUS W. HARRIS · SHEILA FRAZIER
CHARLES McGREGOR · Music Composed and Arranged by CURTIS MAYFIELD · Screenplay by PHILLIP FENTY · Produced
by SIG SHORE · Directed by GORDON PARKS, JR. · from Warner Bros., a Warner Communications company **R**
COPYRIGHT ©1972 WARNER BROS., INC.

72/319

**Superfly** (1972)
US 41 × 27 in. (104 × 69 cm)
Courtesy of the Tony Nourmand Collection

*Shaft* sparked an explosion of blaxploitation films; between 1971 and 1975, over 200 titles were released. Featuring an outstanding score by composer Curtis Mayfield, *Superfly* remains one of the most famous.

Although clearly inspired by *Sweetback*, and intended to capitalize on its success, blaxploitation films like *The Mack* and *Superfly* watered down its theme so as to appeal to a wider, mixed-race audience. The Black Panther spirit was largely replaced by humour and generic sex and violence, and the political passion in these later films was noticeably less fervent. The films themselves proved hugely divisive in the black community. The National Association for the Advancement of Coloured People condemned them as destructive and degrading and it was, in fact, the NAACP that first coined the term 'blaxploitation' to define what they perceived to be the exploitation of black people. On the other hand, the Black Panther movement made *Sweetback* compulsory viewing for all its new recruits. Ever since its emergence, opinion has remained divided as to whether blaxploitation ultimately empowered or repressed black America.

**The Mack** (1973)
US 41 × 27 in. (104 × 69 cm)
Courtesy of the Tony Nourmand Collection

**Cleopatra Jones** (1973)
US 41 × 27 in. (104 × 69 cm)
(Style A)
Courtesy of the Tony Nourmand Collection

Blaxploitation did not confine itself to masculine heroes. Heroines like Pam Grier and Tamara Dobson were soon moving energetically into the same territory. *Cleopatra Jones* and *Foxy Brown* are two of the most famous of a stream of female-empowered movies. Epitomising the strong, sexy, independent woman, Pam Grier continues to be recognized as blaxploitation's ultimate female superstar.

Despite her initial success, Grier, like many in the industry, was hit hard by the sudden end of the blaxploitation cycle in 1975. A number of factors contributed to the genre's rapid demise, but the overriding cause was the realization on the part of movie executives that they no longer needed to produce blaxploitation movies in order to appeal to the black market.

When viewing figures for *The Exorcist* (1973) were analyzed, it was revealed that over one third of the audience was black. Studios soon decided that targeting a market based purely on race had become a dispensable strategy and Hollywood's doors slammed shut on the blaxploitation industry. However, the genre still continues to fascinate and influence filmmakers. Most notably Quentin Tarantino's *Jackie Brown* (1997) not only revived Pam Grier's acting career, but its timeless score and go-getting attitude paid homage to blaxploitation cinema, re-awakening cross-racial interest in the genre.

**Foxy Brown** (1974)
US 60 × 40 in. (152 × 102 cm)
Courtesy of the Tony Nourmand Collection

**Barbarella** (1968)
British 30 × 40 in. (76 × 102 cm)
Art by Robin Ray
Courtesy of The Reel Poster Gallery

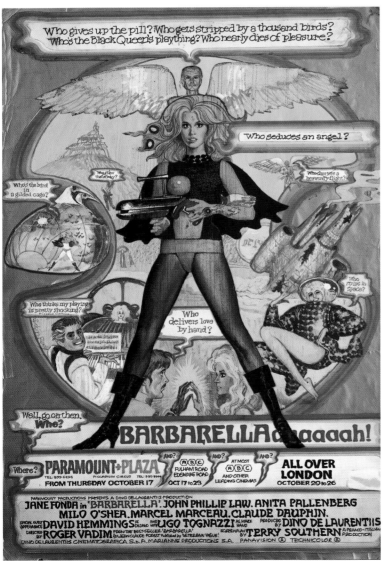

**Barbarella** (1968)
British 26 × 17 in. (66 × 43 cm)
Original Artwork. Mixed media on board. Signed middle left.
Art by Robin Ray
Courtesy of the Haldane Collection

*Barbarella* was classic exploitation but on a bigger budget. The themes of space travel and societies of the future were just an excuse to indulge in plentiful nudity and sex in the fun-filled 60s. The British poster campaign reflects the sexual revolution that was a major feature of the decade. Indeed, the designer of the British artwork, Robin Ray, won the title of Erotic Artist of the Year in 2001. That said, it is interesting to compare Ray's artwork with the finished poster, where all nudity and explicit innuendo were eliminated to satisfy the not-so-fun-filled British Board of Film Censorship.

The 'King of the Czech Comics', **Kaja Saudek** (b. 1935), who was renowned for his brilliant work in the field of adult comic books, was an obvious choice as artist for the Czechoslovakian poster. One of Saudek's most famous creations is a science-fiction epic featuring a winged beauty, Muriel, which was very obviously influenced by the original creator of *Barbarella*, Jean Claude Forest. Incidentally, Saudek modelled Muriel on Bridget Bardot, one-time wife of *Barbarella* director Rodger Vadim.

**Barbarella** (1968)
Czechoslovakian 33 × 23 in. (84 × 58 cm)
Art by Kaja Saudek
Courtesy of the Mo Sheikh-Kadir Collection

**I Married A Monster From Outer Space** (1958)
US 81 × 41 in. (206 × 104 cm)
Courtesy of the Tony Nourmand Collection

In the 50s it was not just the traditional exploitation industry that could see the business potential of the new teenage market that had been borne out of the unprecedented wealth of post-war America. In the mid-50s, **Samuel Z. Arkoff** (1918–2001) and **James H. Nicholson** (1916–1972) formed American International Pictures and began churning out 'B' movies that were a massive success on the drive-in circuit. They focused on teen interest films and most plots centred on juvenile delinquency, science fiction or horror. The shocking, thrilling elements were emphasized to pull in the crowds and the posters often promised more than the films delivered. Indeed, Arkoff and Nicholson would often start with a title, design the poster and only then, if it still looked good, would they go ahead with a script. Many of Hollywood's top names, including Woody Allen, Jack Nicholson and Martin Scorsese began their careers at AIP.

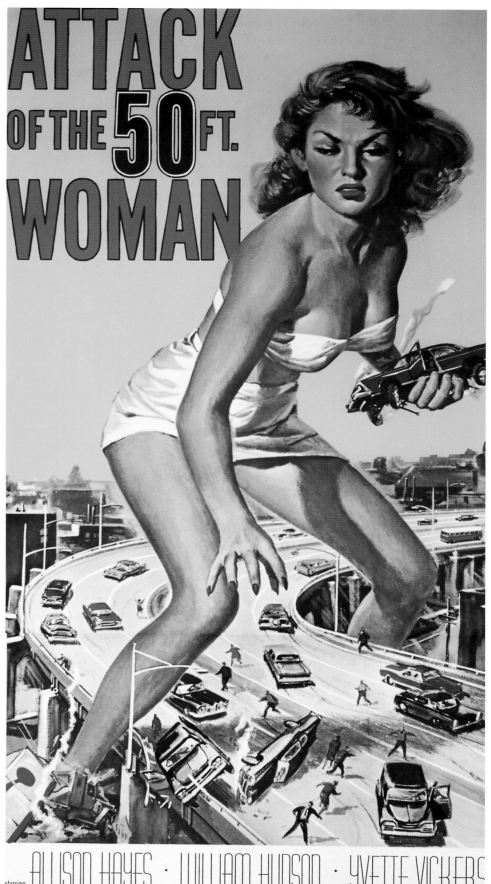

**Attack Of The 50 Foot Woman** (1958)
US 81 × 41 in. (206 × 104 cm)
Art by Reynold Brown
Courtesy of the Haldane Collection

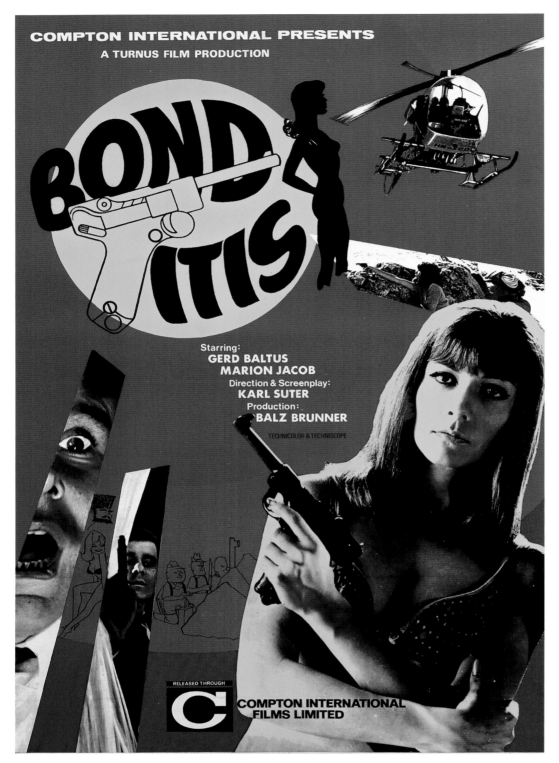

For over forty years, James Bond has proved to be a phenomenal success. Spoofs like *Bonditis* and *Carry On Spying* have ridden on the back of this, exploiting the sub-genre for all its earning potential.

The British poster for *Carry On Spying* was designed by the prolific **Tom William Chantrell** (1916–2001). Chantrell, who created the imagery for many horror posters, was also known for his characteristic depiction of sexuality. His style was perfect for the innuendo-packed series of *Carry On* films.

**Bonditis** (1968)
US 41 × 27 in. (104 × 69 cm)
Courtesy of the Tony Nourmand Collection

**Carry On Spying** (1965)
British 41 × 27 in. (104 × 69 cm)
Art by Tom William Chantrell

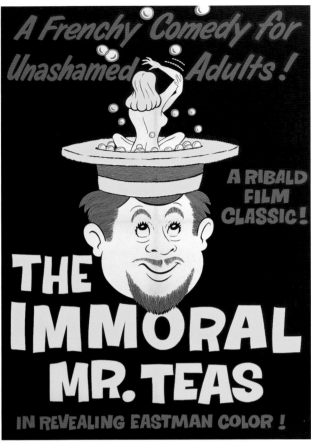

**The Immoral Mr. Teas** (1959)
US 42 × 28 in. (107 × 71 cm)
(Style B)
Courtesy of the Tony Nourmand Collection

**Wild Gals Of The Naked West** (1962)
US 42 × 28 in. (106 × 71cm)
Courtesy of The X-rated Collection

**Russ Meyer** (1922–2004) has been called both 'the Fellini of the sex industry' and 'the Einstein of sex films' – tributes to the man who revolutionized exploitation and launched the 'nudie cutie' sexploitation genre of the 60s. Meyer began making amateur films in his early teens and was winning prizes for his work before he was fifteen. He was a combat photographer during the Second World War and, on his return, worked freelance in Hollywood, doing the stills for *Guys And Dolls* (1955) and *Giant* (1956). Around this time, he also started working in nude photography, an area in which he was particularly skilled. The popularity of his images led to work for *Playboy*, where he was responsible for eight of the first twelve centre-fold spreads.

He made his feature-length directorial debut in 1959 with *The Immoral Mr. Teas*. His old army buddies had put up most of the budget for the film and he cast one of them, his good friend Bill Teas, in the starring role. Influenced by Jacques Tati's *Mr Hulot's Holiday*, it was a fun-filled romp with the added bonus of abundant female nudity. It was the first soft-core sex film to make a profit at the box office and served to illustrate the increasing futility of the Hays Code. It combined humour, nudity and innuendo in a bold, unapologetic way – exploitation no longer had to hide behind a cloak of redeeming moral worth or educational merit. Meyer stuck to the same formula with *Wild Gals Of The Naked West* and *Eve And The Handyman* and the poster art for the three films reflects their ribald content.

**Eve And The Handyman** (1961)
US 42 × 28 in. (107 × 71 cm)
Courtesy of the Tony Nourmand Collection

**Motor Psycho** (1965)
US 41 × 27 in. (104 × 69 cm)
Courtesy of the Tony Nourmand Collection

By the mid-60s, with so many of Meyer's imitators churning out endless variations on the same theme, the box office pulling power of the 'nudie cutie' began to decline. It was at this point that Meyer started adding increasing violence to his films. *Faster Pussycat! Kill! Kill!* and *Motor Psycho* are two of his most memorable and celebrated works from this period. Unlike the majority of his titles, *Motor Psycho* focused on three male protagonists. This was a commercial decision made in an attempt to evade the censors who had started a renewed attack on the nudie flick.

A drive-in hit, *Motor Psycho* consisted of simple action and violence. *Faster Pussycat!* was conceived as a sister film and focused on three violent female protagonists.

The posters for Meyer's films reflect the changes that took place in his work: from the comical, caricature-like, tongue-in-cheek style of the early posters to the, thrilling, electrifying, racy pitch of the later ones.

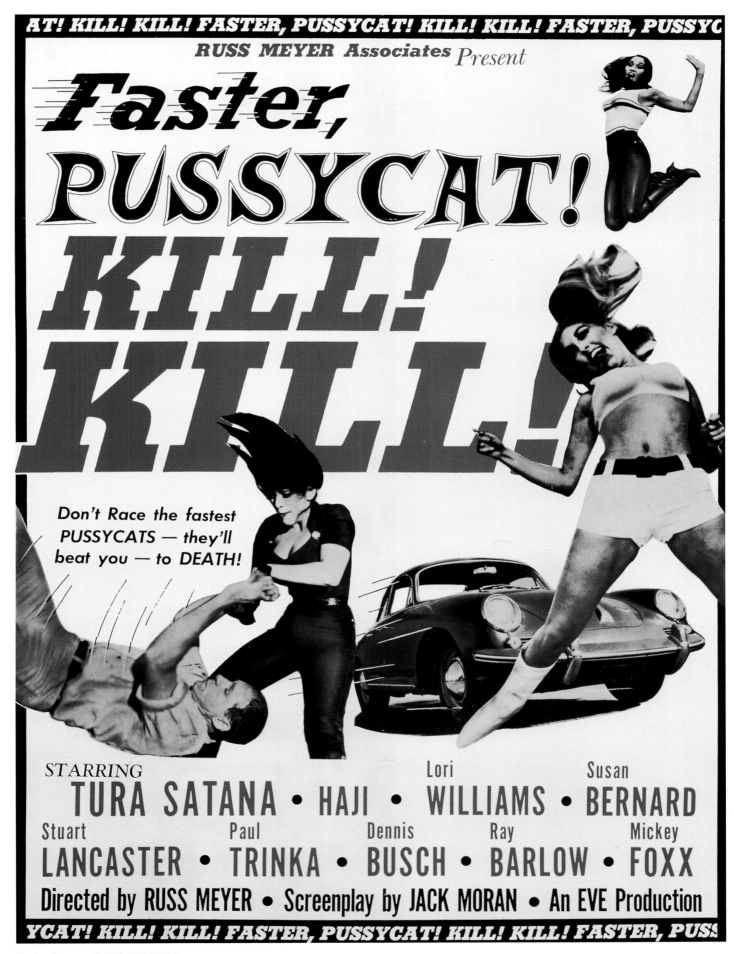

**Faster Pussycat! Kill! Kill!** (1966)
US 41 × 27 in. (104 × 69 cm)
(Style B)
Courtesy of the Tony Nourmand Collection

**Mondo Topless** (1966)
British 30 × 40 in. (76 × 102 cm)
Signed by Russ Meyer in blue felt.
First British release c.1980s.
Courtesy of the Tony Nourmand Collection

Abnormally large-breasted women are one of the trademarks of Meyer films. While this obsession is alluded to on the poster for *Vixen!*, it is blatantly flaunted on the poster for *Mondo Topless* and *Supervixens* (page 190). His well-endowed ladies were undoubtedly one of the key factors that led to the mainstream success of *Vixen!* in 1968. Grossing over 2000 times its cost, it was both a box office and a critical success. Meyer caught the attention of Twentieth Century Fox and the studio hired him to make *Beyond The Valley Of The Dolls* (1970). Although this film also proved to be a hit, Meyer did not enjoy the rigidity of the studio system; he returned to making his own movies in the mid-70s.

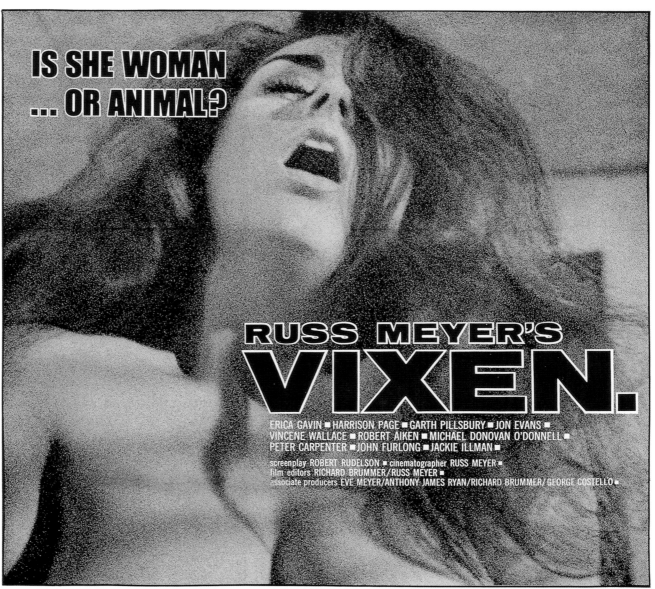

**Vixen!** (1968)
US 41 × 27 in. (104 × 69 cm)
Courtesy of the Tony Nourmand Collection

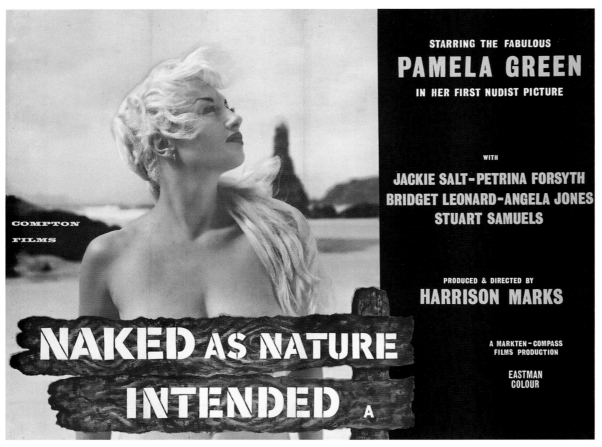

**Naked As Nature Intended** (1961)
British 30 × 40 in. (76 × 102 cm)
Photo by George Harrison Marks
Courtesy of the Tony Nourmand Collection

**Come Play With Me** (1970)
British 30 × 40 in. (76 × 102 cm)
Art by Tom William Chantrell
Courtesy of the Tony Nourmand Collection

Britain's answer to Russ Meyer, **George Harrison Marks** (1926–1997), remains one of Britain's most famous exploitation or 'nudie' directors. Starting out as a photographer at a local theatre, Marks moved to London in the early 50s in a bid to further his career in this field. In 1953, he met the stunning Pamela Green and thus began his career in glamour photography and film. Green and Marks moved in together and started a business selling black and white nude postcards. The cards proved so popular that they launched *Kamera*, a monthly magazine featuring 32 pages of nude glamour photographs. Around this time, Marks also began making films, sticking to the subject he knew best: female nudity. *Naked As Nature Intended* starred Green in the lead role and was one of his first and most popular films. Although the poster itself modestly hides Green's assets, the film was not so shy and proved popular on the 'B' movie circuit. Five years later, Marks was so well-known that he could use his own name to help sell his films, as with *The Naked World Of Harrison Marks*. He commissioned the reputable English illustrator, Tom William Chantrell to design the British poster for *Come Play With Me*. Chantrell had been responsible for the artwork on numerous top Hollywood studio posters, and his was a well-respected name in the world of film poster graphics; the fact that Marks managed to secure such talent to promote his projects is further testament to his success.

Join
the "Dream-In"
and take a "Trip" through

# THE NAKED WORLD OF HARRISON MARKS

PAMELA GREEN    Featuring    JUNE PALMER
CHRIS WILLIAMS    JUTKA GOZ    ANNETTE JOHNSON
CHRIS BROMFIELD        KEN HAYES
DEREK NICHOLS        DAVID ROBERTS

and
GEORGE HARRISON MARKS
Plus twenty beautiful girls

In Glorious Color

**The Naked World Of Harrison Marks** (1965)
US 41 × 27 in. (104 × 69 cm)
Photo by George Harrison Marks
Courtesy of the Tony Nourmand Collection

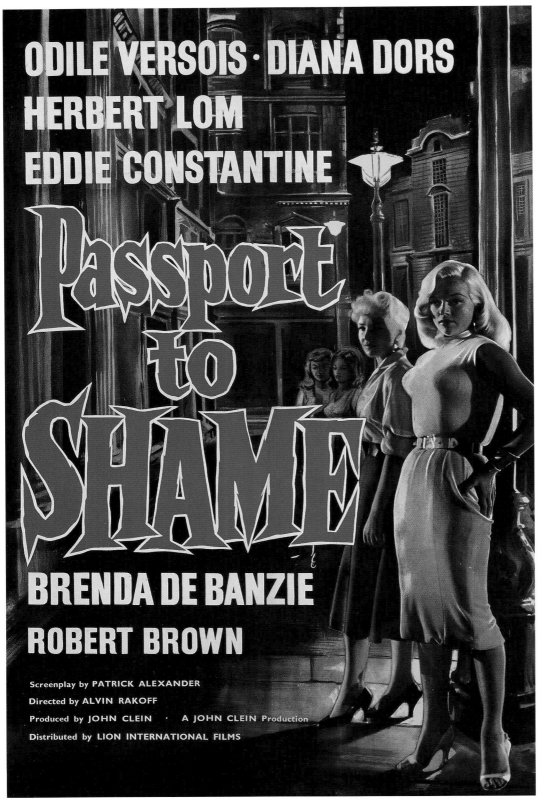

**Passport To Shame** (1958)
British 41 × 27 in. (104 × 69 cm)
Courtesy of the Tony Nourmand Collection

If Harrison Marks was Britain's Russ Meyer, **Diana Dors** (1931–1984) was its Marilyn Monroe. Taken to the movies and given dance lessons from a young age, Diana Mary Fluck became obsessed with Hollywood in her early teens. Looking older than her years, she entered a beauty contest at fourteen, giving her age as seventeen. She won a prize and her photo was printed in the local paper. This led to weekly work as a photographer's model which, in turn, led to her involvement in local theatrical productions. When she was still only fourteen, she gained a place at the London Academy of Music and Dramatic Arts; she was the youngest full-time student they had ever accepted. To help fund her way through college, she posed nude for art shots, still lying about her age. The same glamorous and seductive look that made her popular with photographers, secured her her first film role in *The Shop At Sly Corner* (1947) where she was given a small part as a sexy coquette. It was at this point that she changed her name to Diana Dors. In the mid-40s, she started working with J. Arthur Rank and starred in a number of his films. By the 50s, she was a household name, but despite her varied and competent acting skills, she was almost always typecast as the sexy siren of the piece – as in *Passport To Shame* and *Blonde Sinner*. Diana Dors died an untimely death at the age of 53.

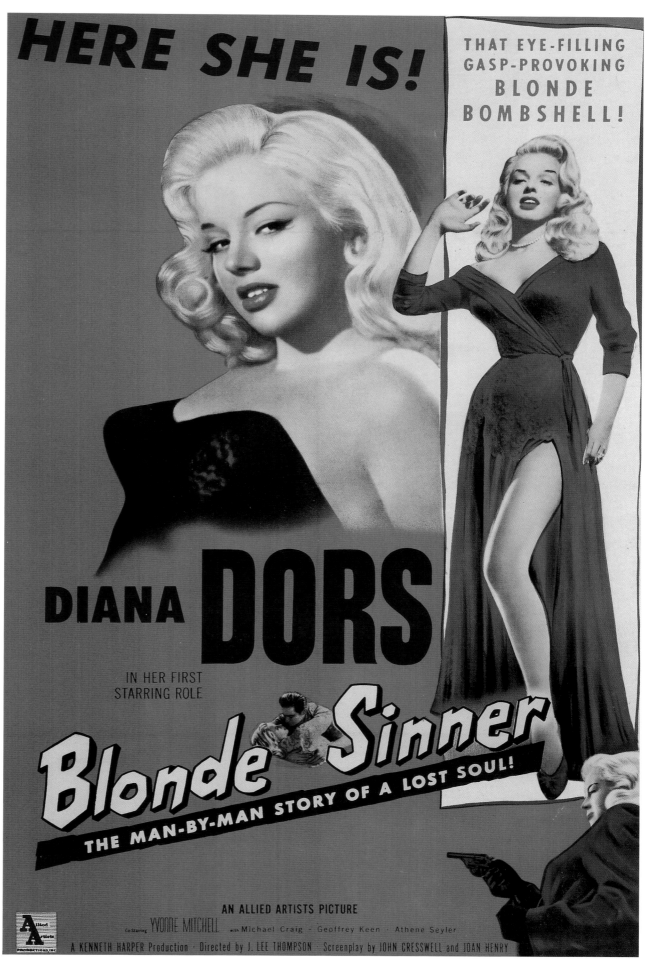

**Yield To The Night (Blonde Sinner)** (1956)
US 41 × 27 in. (104 × 69cm)
Courtesy of the Tony Nourmand Collection

**The Blonde Captive** (1932)
US 41 × 27 in. (104 × 69 cm)
Courtesy of the Tony Nourmand Collection

Unashamed racism was endemic in 30s American society. This was reflected in the movie industry where African-American actors were almost always confined to the roles of servants, 'mammies', jungle-dwelling 'natives' or villains. The prevalent fears of other races 'infiltrating' white society were echoed in films like *The Blonde Captive*. This kind of racism was not confined to the exploitation industry; Universal Studios' *Captive Wild Woman* played upon the same paranoid anxieties – with a gorilla representing the black man, the film was a crude parable about the supposed 'hazards' of attempting to integrate the black and white races. The cycle of jungle epics that emerged in both mainstream and exploitation cinema in this decade is a disturbing reminder of the all-pervading, destructive prejudices that tainted this period of history – prejudices that sadly continue to filter through today.

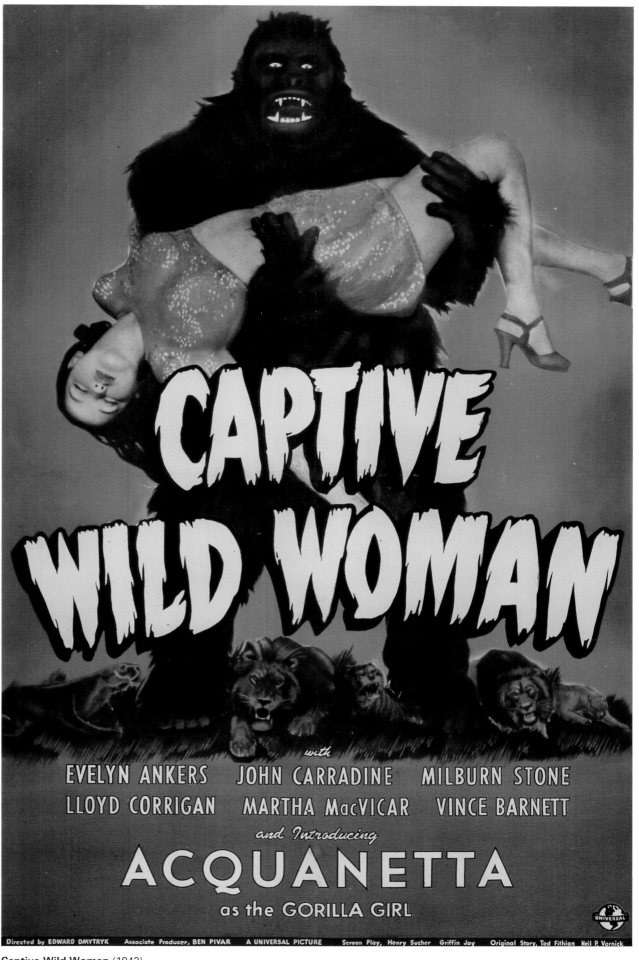

**Captive Wild Woman** (1943)
US 41 × 27 in. (104 × 69 cm)
Courtesy of the Tony Nourmand Collection

**Ingagi** (1931)
US 81 × 41 in. (206 × 104 cm)
Courtesy of The Reel Poster Gallery

The film that started the 30s cycle of jungle epics was *Ingagi*. Made in 1930, it combined film shot in Los Angeles Zoo with old expedition footage. *Ingagi* was presented as a simple ethnographic documentary and ran into controversy after the publication of accusations that scenes had been faked. Incredibly, many people believed that this tale, which involved a gorilla having sex with indigenous women and which featured hitherto unknown jungle creatures, was based on fact. An investigation was launched. The unknown creatures, it was revealed, were turtles with mocked-up wings and tails, the 'pygmies' were Californian children from the local neighbourhood, and, most painfully, much of the documentary footage had been stolen from the 1914 film, *Heart Of Africa*. Unsurprisingly, the film's producers were sued, but the scandal only served to boost ratings. *Ingagi* played on the exploitation circuit for several years.

**Wild Women Of Borneo** (1931)
US 41 × 27 in. (104 × 69 cm)
Courtesy of the Hastings Collection

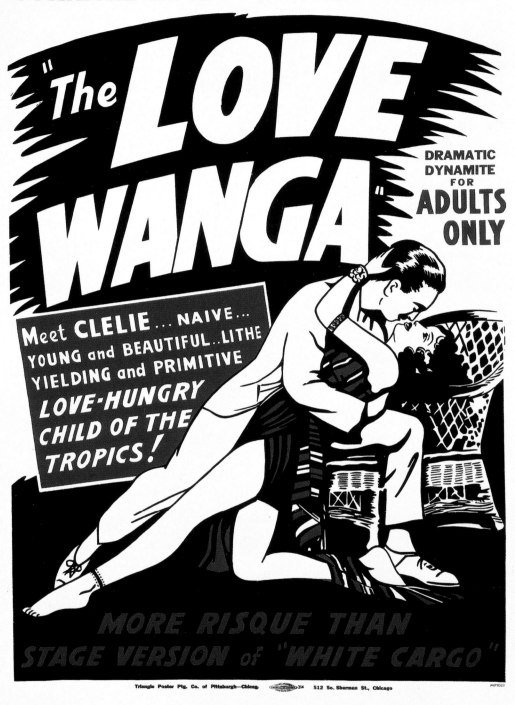

**Ouanga (The Love Wanga)** (1936)
US 41 × 27 in. (104 × 69 cm)

*Forbidden Adventure* had been entitled *Angkor* until renamed by Dwain Esper in a bid to appeal to a wider audience. It tells the story of a group of explorers who set off in search of the lost city of Angkor in Cambodia. With its inevitable melange of love-crazed gorillas and topless women, the film follows the typical jungle-epic formula. *Forbidden Adventure* was concocted by combining old footage of a Harvard expedition with added scenes of men dressed in gorilla suits cavorting with naked ladies.

**Angkor (Forbidden Adventure)** (1935)
US 41 × 27 in. (104 × 69 cm)
Courtesy of the Tony Nourmand Collection

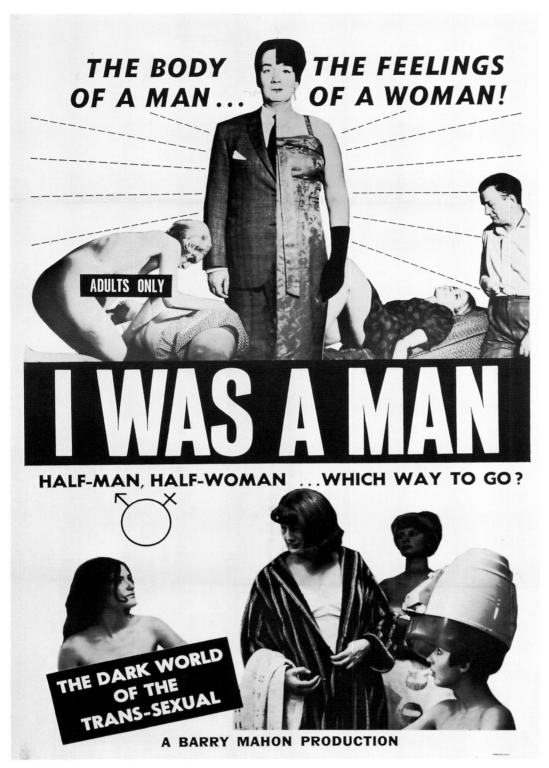

**I Was A Man** (1967)
US 41 × 27 in. (104 × 69 cm)
Courtesy of the Tony Nourmand Collection

In February 1953, George Jorgenson became famous as the first American to publicly admit to undergoing a sex-change operation. George became Christine and the press had a field day with his/her story. Always quick to seize upon the scandal *de jour*, the exploitation industry followed suit. In the same year, *Glen Or Glenda*, a film detailing the life story of a transvestite, was released. It was written and directed by the infamous **Ed Wood Jr.** (1924–1978), who also played the starring role. The film was Wood's directorial debut and its theme was particularly relevant as he himself was a cross-dresser (he is reputed to have worn a bra and panties underneath his Marine Corps uniform during the Second World War). In 1994 Tim Burton directed an insightful biopic of Wood who has been labelled 'the worst director of all time'. He died penniless and unknown, yet his films maintain a cult following.

**Glen Or Glenda** (1953)
US 41 × 27 in. (104 × 69 cm)
Courtesy of the Hastings Collection

The more sensational aspects of mental illness, like drugs, sex and violence, were meat and drink to the exploitation filmmakers and two films from the 60s explored the themes of sanity and madness. The sensationalist poster for *Shock Corridor* belies a surprisingly sophisticated film. Dismissed at the time as trash, it was a key factor in director Samuel Fuller's banishment from Hollywood. It has since been recognized as an important and influential work, inspiring the films of Martin Scorsese, Quentin Tarantino and Jim Jarmusch amongst others. *Shock Corridor* often seems lurid and excessive yet Fuller used the arena of an insane asylum to make an astute comment on American society.

*The Chapman Report* also explored the frontiers of sanity. It was based on the best-selling book of the same name by Irving Wallace, which in turn had been inspired by Alfred Kinsey's reports on human sexual behaviour, much publicized in the late 40s.

**Shock Corridor** (1963)
US 36 × 14 in. (91 × 36 cm)
Courtesy of the Tony Nourmand Collection

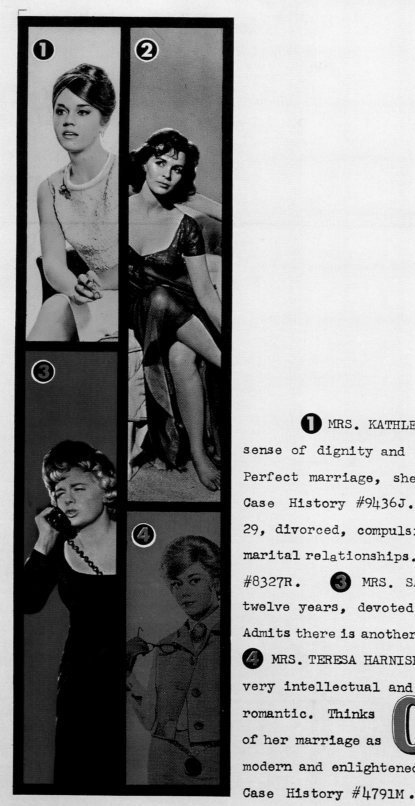

**1** MRS. KATHLEEN BALLARD: 26, widowed, sense of dignity and poise. War-hero husband. Perfect marriage, she says. Obviously lying. Case History #9436J. **2** MRS. NAOMI SHIELDS: 29, divorced, compulsive self-hate for extra-marital relationships. Needs help. Case History #8327R. **3** MRS. SARA GARNELL: 34, married twelve years, devoted wife and mother of two. Admits there is another man. Case History #3721B. **4** MRS. TERESA HARNISH: 28, very intellectual and very romantic. Thinks of her marriage as modern and enlightened. Case History #4791M.

A DARRYL F. ZANUCK PRODUCTION **The Chapman Report**

**THE PERSONAL STORY BEHIND A SEX SURVEY...FROM THE CONTROVERSIAL BEST SELLING NOVEL.**

STARRING
EFREM ZIMBALIST, JR. · SHELLEY WINTERS · JANE FONDA · CLAIRE BLOOM · GLYNIS JOHNS · RAY DANTON · TY HARDIN · ANDREW DUGGAN · **WB**
JOHN DEHNER · Directed by GEORGE CUKOR · Based on the novel by IRVING WALLACE · Produced by RICHARD D. ZANUCK · Music by Leonard Rosenman · Screenplay by WYATT COOPER and DON M. MANKIEWICZ · **TECHNICOLOR® FROM WARNER BROS.**

*No one under 16 will be admitted unless accompanied by an adult.*

**The Chapman Report** (1962)
US 41 × 27 in. (104 × 69 cm)
Courtesy of the Tony Nourmand Collection

**She Freak** (1967)
US 41 × 27 in. (104 × 69 cm)
Courtesy of the Tony Nourmand Collection

**Chained For Life** (1951)
US 60 × 40 in. (152 × 102 cm)
Courtesy of the Tony Nourmand Collection

Human oddities and deformities have always fascinated certain sections of the public and the film industry soon found an opportunity to exploit this morbid interest. Released in 1932, Tod Browning's *Freaks* featured a cast of carnival people. Browning's use of real-life 'freaks' so revolted and disgusted critics and audiences that the film effectively ended his career and nearly destroyed MGM. Rejected by Hollywood, this taboo film provided a commercial opportunity for Dwain Esper: in the late 30s he bought the print and proceeded to tour the picture for several years under a number of titles. To satisfy audiences hungry for more than just a circus act, Esper also inserted an extra square-up reel of nudity at the end of the film. Twenty years later, two of the stars of *Freaks*, the Siamese twins Daisy and Violet Hilton, starred in their own full-length flick, *Chained For Life*. The market for the weird and wonderful had still not abated in the late 60s when legendary exploitation giants David F. Friedman and Dan Sonney released *She Freak* – a film that blended sex, horror and the grotesque.

**David F. Friedman** (b. 1923) had learnt the exploitation trade at an early age and had toured with Kroger Babb and his *Mom And Dad* epic in the 40s. In the 50s, Friedman secured a job as a publicist at Paramount, but gave it up to pursue his career in independent films. In the early 60s, he joined forces with Herschell Gordon Lewis and together they pioneered the 'Gore' genre of excess violence and sex. After leaving Lewis, Friedman approached Dan Sonney with whom he produced an endless stream of exploitation fodder. Essentially a remake of *Freaks*, the theme of *She Freak* was particularly appropriate for Friedman as he had begun his career in the carnival trade.

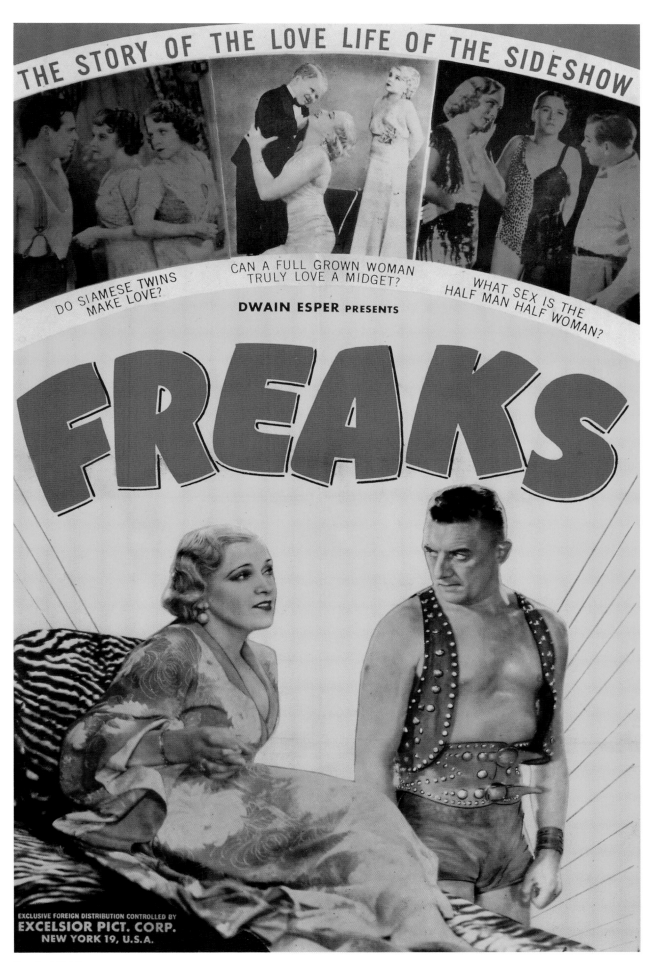

**Freaks** (1932)
US 41 × 27 in. (104 × 69 cm)
(Re-release 1949)
Courtesy of the Tony Nourmand Collection

**Polyester** (1981)
US 41 × 27 in. (104 × 69 cm)
Courtesy of the Tony Nourmand Collection

Known as the 'Sultan of Sleaze', **John Waters** (b. 1946) is notorious for his taboo-breaking films. Yet his work, unlike that of many exploitation directors, is recognized as being an intelligent, carefully observed commentary on society. His films may be gory, gross and extreme but they are infused with a savvy black humour. His uncompromising portrayal of abortion, the Church, drugs, sex and perversion (which included images of transsexuals eating dog excrement) was instrumental in redefining the boundaries of what was acceptable on screen. Waters' gritty approach to filmmaking has influenced a number of directors.

Waters openly admits that he himself was obsessed with violence and debauchery from an early age. He was given a camera when he was seventeen and used the opportunity to explore these facets of his own character in a creative way, beginning to make short films with his misfit friends. Waters' first feature film was *Mondo Trasho* (1969) and he was arrested on obscenity charges before the premiere. This only boosted his reputation and after the release of *Pink Flamingos* (1972) and *Desperate Living*, his underground success was guaranteed.

*Polyester* marked Waters' first move into mainstream cinema. Only slightly less extreme than his earlier work, it still contained all the classic Waters trademarks. *Polyester* was originally shown in 'Odorama' – the audience were given cards to 'scratch and sniff' at appropriate points throughout the film. This sort of exploitation gimmick was borrowed from one of Waters' influences, William Castle. *Polyester* also featured a theme song by Chris Stein and Debbie Harry.

**Tino Avelli** (b. 1938) was born in Tripoli and moved to Rome, the epicentre of Italian design, after graduating with an art degree. He works in advertising and has designed film posters for almost all the major American studios. The poster for *Desperate Living* illustrates his particular skill in observing faces and expressions.

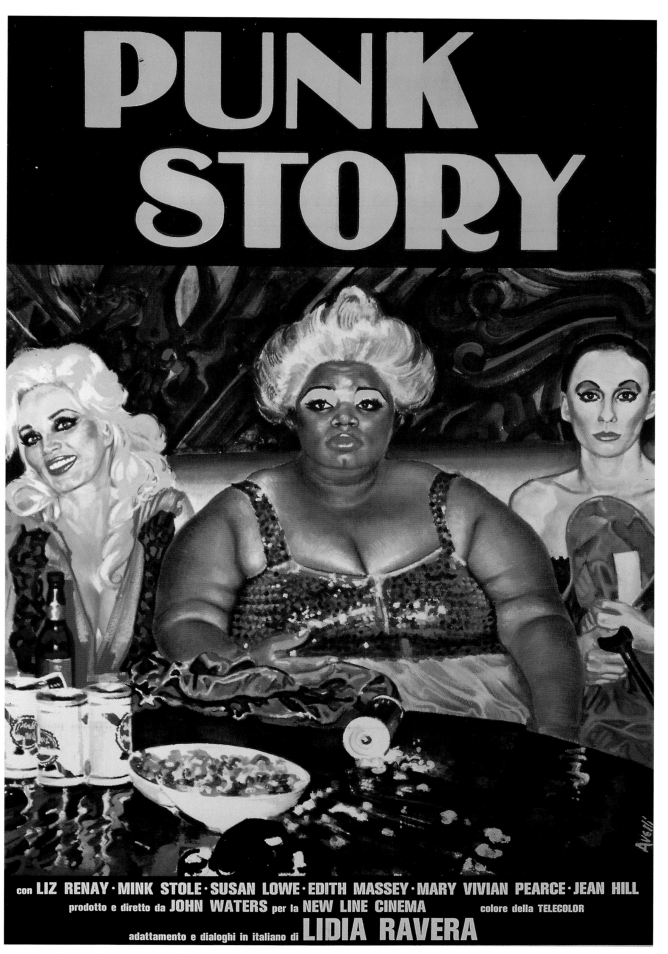

**Desperate Living (Punk Story)** (1977)
Italian 55 × 39 in. (140 × 99 cm)
Art by Tino Avelli
Courtesy of the Tony Nourmand Collection

"**We're not rated X for nothin', baby!**"

**FRITZ the CAT** X

Jerry Gross Presents • "FRITZ THE CAT" • A Steve Krantz Production • Based upon characters created by R CRUMB • Screenplay by RALPH BAKSHI • Directed by RALPH BAKSHI • Produced by STEVE KRANTZ • A Cinemation Industries Release • Original Soundtrack Album on Fantasy Records
© Aurica Finance Company, N.V. 1972.

*He's X rated and animated!*

**Fritz The Cat** (1972)
US 28 × 18 in. (71 × 46 cm)
Art by Robert Crumb
Courtesy of the Tony Nourmand Collection

The innocent field of animation seems far removed from the world of exploitation, yet as early as the 20s Hollywood was adding a sexual element to cartoons in a bid to attract larger audiences, as the provocatively titled *Sax Appeal* demonstrates. Conversely, in the 70s, *Fritz The Cat* may have lacked a suggestive title but it was unashamedly devoted to the topics of sex, drugs and violence and was the first animated film to be given an X certificate.

The film was based on the underground comic strip of the same name created by **Robert Crumb** (b. 1943). As a boy, Crumb had made his own comic books and devised a strip based on his household pet, Fred, who was the model for the famous Fritz. Living in California, Crumb soon established his reputation as a comic-book artist and he gained a strong cult following with his magazine *Zap*. Crumb embodied the counter-culture hippie movement of the period. Through his irreverent, drug-taking, orgy-partaking characters, he provided an important social commentary on society and the Establishment.

In the late 60s, the animator Ralph Bakshi approached Crumb with the idea of turning *Fritz The Cat* into a film. Although the end result was a commercial success, Crumb hated it and killed off the character in his comic strip as a result.

**Sax Appeal** (1927)
US 41 × 27 in. (104 × 69 cm)
Courtesy of the Roberto Hoornweg Collection

**Jag r Nyfiken – En Film I Gult (I Am Curious (Yellow))** (1967)
Japanese 30 × 20 in. (76 × 51 cm)
(Style A)
Courtesy of the Tony Nourmand Collection

*I Am Curious (Yellow)* was a controversial mix of sex and politics. Made in Sweden, it was seized at customs upon its arrival in the US. After a lengthy and much publicized court case, the film was finally granted approval on the grounds that it was an 'intellectual effort'. Despite the weak story line, the filmmakers' motives were noble and the film made a valid attempt at social commentary. Even the advertising for the movie avoided the promotional techniques normally used for sex films: the American poster does not even hint at the film's portrayal of full frontal male and female nudity.

# I Am Curious
### (yellow)

Vilgot Sjöman's complete and uncut *I Am Curious (Yellow)* is "a landmark likely to permanently shatter many of our last remaining movie conventions," says William Wolf of Cue Magazine. The Evergreen Film presented by Grove Press stars Lena Nyman and is a Sandrews Production.
ADMISSION IS RESTRICTED TO ADULTS.

**Jag r Nyfiken – En Film I Gult (I Am Curious (Yellow))** (1967)
US 41 × 27 in. (104 × 69 cm)
Courtesy of the Tony Nourmand Collection

**Emmanuelle** (1974)
US 41 × 27 in. (104 × 69 cm)
(Advance)
Design by Steve Frankfurt
Courtesy of the Tony Nourmand Collection

The 70s were the golden era of the soft porn movie. More money was being poured into the industry than ever before and as a result, a more sophisticated product was being created. In 1972, *Deep Throat* was released and for the first time, an X-rated movie was being shown in mainstream cinemas. 1972 also saw the release of Bertolucci's *Last Tango In Paris*. Although this was not a porn film *per se*, it did feature scenes of an unreservedly adult nature. The lines dividing porn from mainstream cinema were becoming blurred. Films like *Deep Throat*, *Behind The Green Door* and *Emmanuelle* were attracting a fashionable, young crowd and it became almost trendy for couples to go and see these films together. More significantly perhaps, the movies themselves were receiving critical attention. The term 'porno chic' was coined to describe this phenomenon.

No film represents the spirit of porno chic better than Just Jaeckin's *Emmanuelle*. A French film based on the memoirs of Emmanuelle Arsan, *Emmanuelle* brought a new sense of glamour and class to the genre. With a background in art and sculpture, Jaeckin was well equipped to make what was, by contemporary porn standards, a refined and artistic film – his intention was to create a stylish movie with high production standards that was erotic but never sleazy. By consciously avoiding all the standard clichés of earlier porn films, *Emmanuelle* soon became a renowned *tour de force*.

The publicity material that accompanied *Emmanuelle* reflected the film's ambitions and style. While Richard Suzuki's famous photograph of Sylvia Kristel sitting topless in a chair became the respectable face of the X-rated film industry, Steve Frankfurt's concept for the American poster campaign effectively portrayed the new ethos of porno chic. Frankfurt not only created the subtle, sensual imagery for the American poster, but was also responsible for the notorious tagline: 'X was never quite like this'. The fact that Frankfurt, who was highly regarded in the world of poster design, chose to become involved in moulding the film's public image was itself a testament to the level of credibility it attained.

By the end of the 70s, with sex being represented more frequently and more openly in mainstream cinema in response to more tolerant social attitudes, it seemed that the underground sexploitation movie had had its day. But this change did not long survive the introduction of video technology in the 80s which dramatically lowered production costs and created a whole new audience who could now watch porn in the privacy of their homes or hotel rooms. The result was that porn was effectively pushed underground once more and quickly re-established itself in the sleazy territory it had occupied so comfortably in the past.

エマニエル夫人

原作「エマニエル・アルサン／アラン・キュニー／マリカ・グリーン」監督ジュスト・ジェーキン／シルビア・クリステル
主題歌・アンヌ・アンデルセン（コロムビア・レコード）フランス映画／日本ヘラルド映画
原作「エマニエル」（二見書房刊）サントラ盤（ワーナー・レコード）
＊あの快感が

**Emmanuelle** (1974)
Japanese 30 × 20 in. (76 × 51 cm)
Photo by Richard Suzuki
Courtesy of the Tony Nourmand Collection

**Mädchen In Uniform (Jeunes Filles En Uniforme / Maidens In Uniform)** (1931)
French 63 × 47 in. (160 × 119 cm)
Art by Carlo Mariani
Courtesy of the Tony Nourmand Collection

Released in 1932, Gustav Machaty's *Extase* became a *cause célèbre*. The film, now recognized as a landmark in European cinema and revolutionary in its enlightened portrayal of female sexuality, stirred up an international scandal and was banned in America. The cause of the furore was that actress Hedy Lamarr (then still Hedy Kiesler) appeared naked for a full ten minutes. The fact that the camera also lingered on a close-up of her face while she was sexually aroused only added to the uproar. **Carlo Mariani** captured the sensuality of this latter image in his artwork for the film's French poster.

The film made a star of Hedy. At the time, she was married to Fritz Mandl, a rich German and a Nazi sympathizer. Unable to endure his wife's notoriety, Mandl tried in vain to buy all copies of the film after its release. He also became increasingly possessive of Hedy – never letting her out of his sight. Isolated and unhappy, the actress finally made her escape by drugging a maid and escaping from their hotel room in disguise. She made her way to America where she quickly became one of Hollywood's most alluring stars. (Interestingly, she was also a gifted electrical engineer and was honoured by the Electronic Frontier Foundation in 1997 for her contribution to society.)

Based on a play by Christa Winsloe, the German-made *Mädchen In Uniform* is one of the earliest films to portray homosexuality. It is the story of the relationship between a young girl and her female teacher at a prestigious boarding school. Although the passionate relationship between the pair is never shown explicitly, it is very clearly implied. When the authoritarian head mistress finds out about the affair she determines to destroy it and her attitude is presented as a microcosm of traditionally oppressive Prussian attitudes. Powerful and absorbing, *Mädchen In Uniform* remains an important historical document and a landmark film. The French poster is again by Carlo Mariani. Working in the 30s, Mariani's distinct, compelling style was influenced by the Art Deco movement.

**Extase (Ecstasy)** (1932)
French 63 × 47 in. (160 × 119 cm)
Art by Carlo Mariani
Courtesy of the Chris Dark Collection

**Nature's Sweethearts** (1963)
US 41 × 27 in. (104 × 69 cm)
Courtesy of the Tony Nourmand Collection

The nudist movement began in Europe in the first decade of the twentieth century. Thirty years later it had spread to America and the film industry was quick to realize that the phenomenon offered a new pretext for showing naked flesh. *The Unashamed*, a tale of lovers in a nudist colony, was one of several pre-Hays Code productions to take advantage of this opportunity. *Nature's Sweethearts* was made a generation later yet featured almost indentical scenes of nudity that were still considered sufficiently titillating to sell tickets.

● **1903**. Richard Ungewitter publishes his vision of a utopian, clothes-free future. 90,000 copies of his book are sold.
● **1903**. The first nudist resort opens in Germany.
● **1932**. The first nudist resort opens in America.

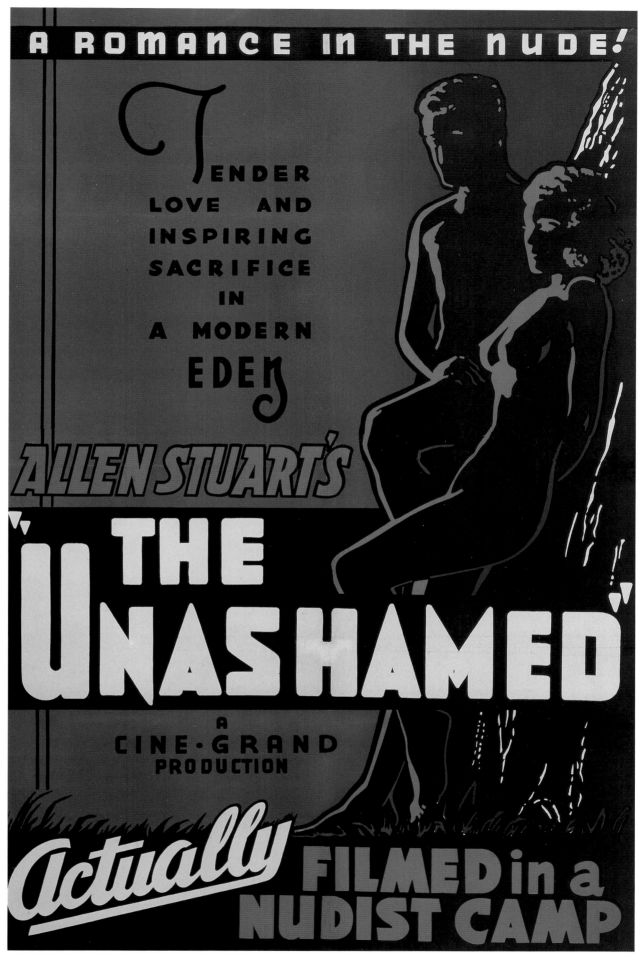

**The Unashamed** (1932)
US 41 × 27 in. (104 × 69 cm)
Courtesy of the Tony Nourmand Collection

**The Strip Tease Murder Case** (1950)
US 41 × 27 in. (104 × 69 cm)
Courtesy of the Tony Nourmand Collection

In the 50s, traditional burlesque theatre was superseded by cinematic striptease shows. Nudity was still the life-blood of exploitation and this new genre offered the roadshow men an easy way to make ends meet. Burlesque films were often marketed as 'old-fashioned' nostalgic entertainment and they featured some of the most famous veterans of the live circuit, including Tempest Storm and Bettie Page.

Known as 'The Fabulous 4D Girl', **Tempest Storm** (b. 1928) was born Annie Blanche Banks and was one of the last classic burlesque stars. She ran away from an abusive home and started out as a chorus girl before moving into the strip world in the late 40s. Known for her luxuriant figure and flaming red hair, Russ Meyer's photographs helped her become a huge pin-up star. Tempest is rumoured to have had affairs with John F. Kennedy and Elvis Presley, and at one point, she had her breasts insured for $50,000.

Another famous pin-up girl, **Bettie Page** (b. 1923), was voted 'Miss Pin-up of the World' in 1955 and was known as 'The Girl With the Perfect Figure'. After graduating with a BA in Education from Peabody College, Page moved to New York where her glamour-modelling career took off. She appeared in numerous magazines, including the centre-fold of *Playboy* and quickly became one of the best-known faces in the business. During the 80s and 90s she developed something of a cult following and today there are endless websites devoted to the dark-haired beauty.

**Teaserama** (1955)
US 41 × 27 in. (104 × 69 cm)
Courtesy of the Tony Nourmand Collection

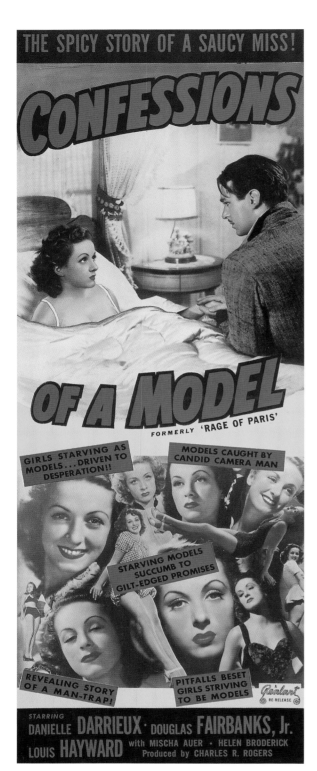

**The Rage Of Paris (Confessions Of A Model)** (1938)
US 36 × 14 in. (91 × 36 cm)
(Re-release 1951)
Courtesy of the Tony Nourmand Collection

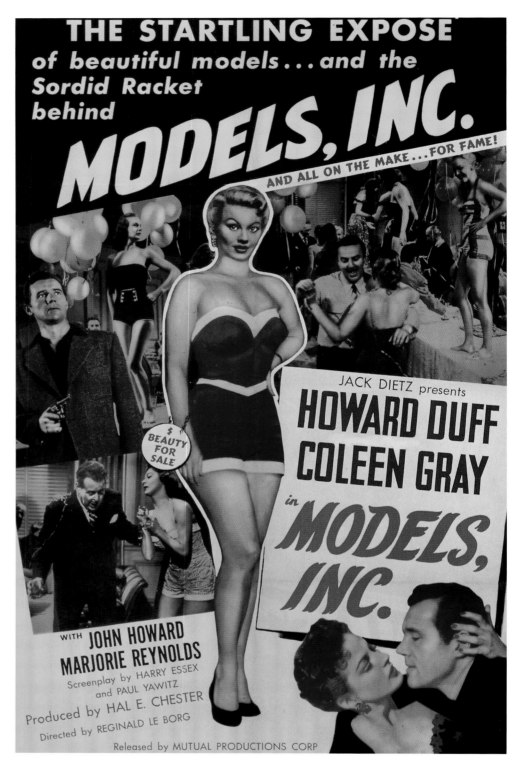

**Models, Inc.** (1952)
US 41 × 27 in. (104 × 69 cm)
Courtesy of the Tony Nourmand Collection

*Confessions Of A Model*, *Models, Inc.* and *Secrets Of A Model* all tell similar tales of an innocent girl selling herself for some much-needed cash. The links between modelling and prostitution are clearly implied: these girls are prepared to compromise their morals indiscriminately in order to make it to the top. The subject matter ensured strong audience appeal, and today's unforgiving tabloid coverage of the underbelly of celebrity life suggests that the public remains as fascinated as ever by such revelations.

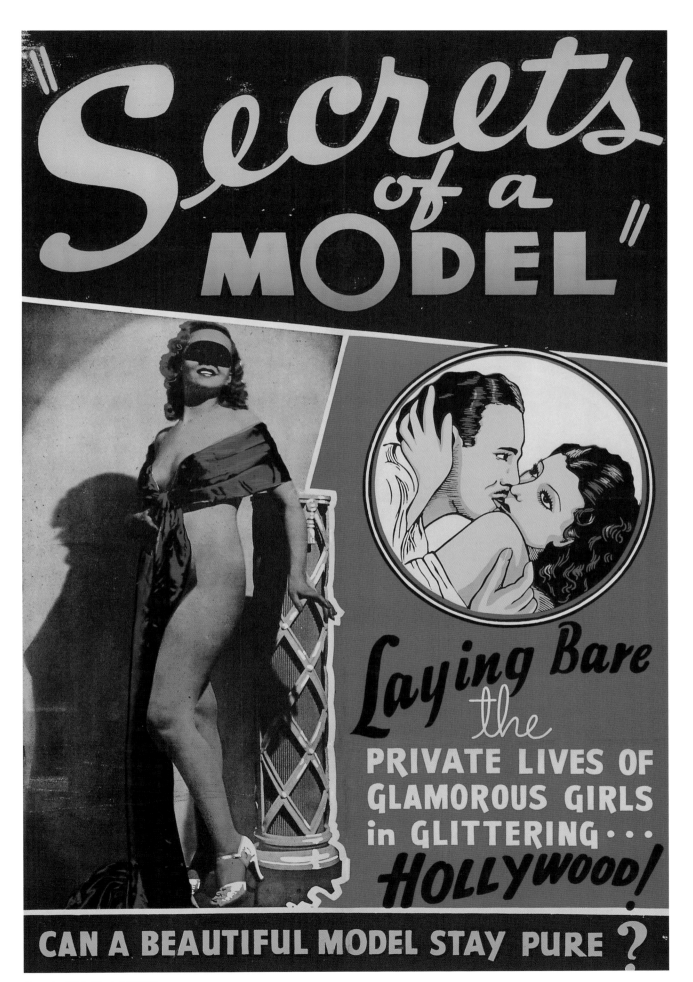

**Secrets Of A Model** (1940)
US 41 × 27 in. (104 × 69 cm)
Courtesy of the Tony Nourmand Collection

THE NEW JAZZ SENSATION

ADULTS ONLY

FLAMING PASSION

STORY of A HIGH SCHOOL GIRL LED INTO A LIFE of SHAME

A TIMELY WARNING TO PARENTS OF TODAY

**Flaming Passion** (c.1930s)
US 81 × 41 in. (206 × 104 cm)
Courtesy of the Tony Nourmand Collection

Independent exploitation films had a long shelf-life; they could be released and re-released under a myriad of different titles to appeal to the same audiences time and time again. Often, a couple of extra reels would be added to an old film so it could be re-marketed as an entirely new product. For this reason, it is sometimes difficult to trace the original title of a film from the advertising material that has survived. The characteristics of the posters for *Flaming Passion* and *Pathway To Hell* place them in the 30s, but their generic images and taglines provide no clues as to the exact date of their release. Like countless other independent exploitation titles, the origins and subsequent metamorphoses of these films remain a mystery.

**Pathway To Hell** (c.1930s)
US 41 × 27 in. (104 × 69 cm)
Courtesy of the Tony Nourmand Collection

**Guilty Parents** (1934)
US 41 × 27 in. (104 × 69 cm)
Courtesy of the Tony Nourmand Collection

*Guilty Parents* was introduced with a 'square-up reel' that denounced sexual ignorance as 'the black plague of adolescence'. The square-up reel was a common feature of exploitation industry films. It was usually characterized by a statement from the film's producer, or an 'expert' in the relevant field, which condemned the immoral nature of the subject matter that was about to be shown. Often used as a means of 'justifying' the exhibition of the film on the grounds of its 'educational' content, the square-up reel stressed the sincerity of the filmmakers' intentions and the necessary service they were providing to the American people by imparting valuable information, which was otherwise denied to them, on topics such as sex, drugs, venereal disease or childbirth.

In reality, of course, the reel was simply a means of circumventing censors and local police, blurring the margins of legality and, perhaps, allowing members of the audience to persuade themselves that they were attending out of an earnest desire for self-improvement.

**Are These Our Parents?** (1944)
US 41 × 27 in. (104 × 69 cm)
Courtesy of the Tony Nourmand Collection

**Tomorrow's Children** (1934)
US 41 × 27 in. (104 × 69 cm)
Courtesy of the Tony Nourmand Collection

● 'It is better for the world, if instead of waiting to execute degenerate offspring for crime or to let them starve for their imbecility, society can prevent those who are manifestly unfit from continuing their kind.' (Supreme Court Justice Oliver Wendell Holmes Jr., after passing the first-ever sentence of sterilization on a woman in 1907.)

Two more 'guilty parent' exploitation flicks of the 30s were *What Becomes Of the Children?* and *Tomorrow's Children*. The latter was significant in that it dealt with the political hot potato of sterilization and tied in with the Eugenics movement's call for the prevention of procreation by the 'unfit'. *Tomorrow's Children* was released the same year that Nazi Germany introduced mass sterilization of the mentally handicapped. At this time, many in America supported such a programme and indeed 27 of the 48 US states sanctioned sterilization by court order. The film was refused a seal on its release – however this was perhaps less to do with the sterilization issue than the fact that the movie was highly critical of the behaviour of the upper classes. *Tomorrow's Children* starred Sterling Holloway who would later become famous as the voice of Winnie the Pooh.

**What Becomes Of The Children?** (1936)
US 41 × 27 in. (104 × 69 cm)
Courtesy of the Tony Nourmand Collection

**Damaged Goods** (1937)
US 41 × 27 in. (104 × 69 cm)
Courtesy of the Tony Nourmand Collection

In the early twentieth century, a significant percentage of America's population was suffering from venereal disease. Although effective medical treatment for syphilis became available from 1909, open discussion of the subject was taboo. As a result there was little or no information available to the public, a state of affairs that was sometimes defended on the grounds that an awareness of effective treatments for syphilis would lead to greater promiscuity.

The first play brave enough to address the problem openly was Eugene Brieux's *Damaged Goods*, which premiered in 1913. Surprisingly, it was a hit with audiences, critics and censors alike. Its success was due to the fact that the play remained very 'clean' and was seen to reinforce, rather than undermine, the prevailing morals of the day. Brieux took the 'Progressive' view that the spread of syphilis could be laid fairly and squarely at the doors of the lower and immigrant classes. As they 'infiltrated' into established American society they introduced this dreadful disease into the hitherto unsullied and innocent ranks of the middle and upper classes.

*Damaged Goods* was made into a film in 1914 and the next four years saw a huge rise in similar movies about the same subject. Meanwhile, public awareness of the scourge of venereal disease was also increasing. Towards the end of the First World War, a series of documentary films dealing with syphilis, originally made for the US Army, were released to the general public. These created a massive backlash and caused a sea change in the opinion of critics and censors. The problem was not so much that the films were overtly graphic, but that they stressed that everyone, irrespective of nationality, class or creed, was at risk of contracting the disease. The implication that the ruling classes were as likely as the lower orders to put themselves at risk by engaging in illicit sexual activity was considered outrageous and the censors reacted by indiscriminately banning all films related to venereal disease. Before long, a small group of men saw the business potential of screening such movies without official sanction. Thus, the exploitation industry was born and the next twenty years saw a flood of films with titles like *Wild Oats*.

By the 30s, public attitudes towards the problem had changed and a national campaign, supported by both rich and poor, was launched to stamp out the disease. The savvy exploitation roadshow men took advantage of this changed atmosphere to release a remake of Brieux's *Damaged Goods*.

**Wild Oats** (c.1920s)
US 41 × 27 in. (104 × 69 cm)

**Bootleg Babies** (1947)
US 41 × 27 in. (104 × 69 cm)
Courtesy of the Tony Nourmand Collection

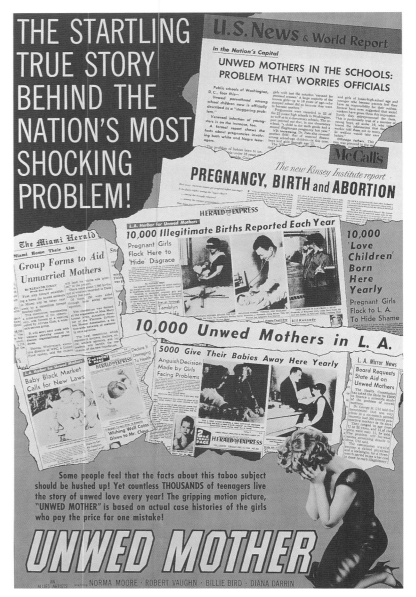

**Unwed Mother** (1958)
US 41 × 27 in. (104 × 69 cm)
Courtesy of the Tony Nourmand Collection

The release of *Unwed Mother* by big-name studio Allied Artists in 1958 was significant in that it showed that mainstream cinema now posed a real threat to the exploitation roadshow men. After the amendments to the Hays Code came into effect in 1956, Hollywood's 'B' studios could once again begin to compete for a major slice of the traditional exploitation market. Ironically, the Forty Thieves provided the big studios with many lessons in advertising techniques; Allied Artists' poster for *Unwed Mother* exhibits the same 'over the top' style as many of the roadshow posters.

From the 50s onwards, as Hollywood began to re-occupy much of the territory it had lost to the roadshow men in the 30s, exploitation itself shifted into a new era, with personalities like Russ Meyer, David Friedman, Dan Sonney and John Waters taking over the reins.

**Black Market Babies** (1945)
US 81 × 41 in. (206 × 104 cm)
Courtesy of the Tony Nourmand Collection

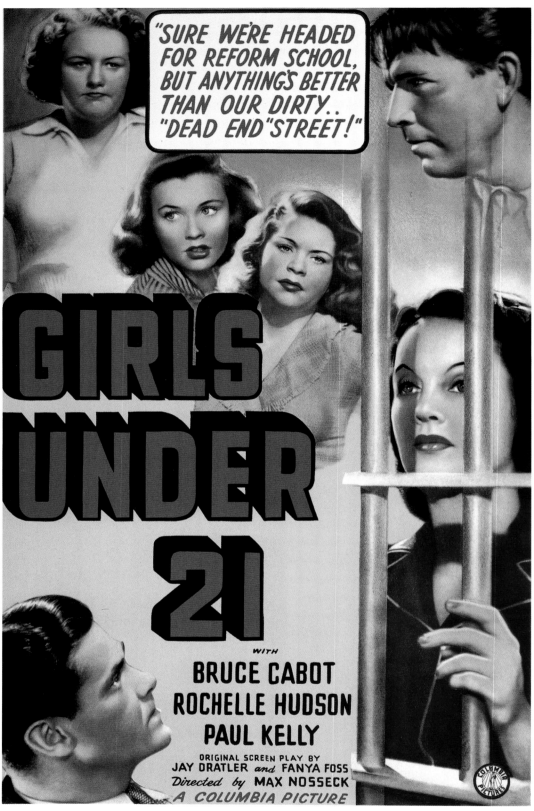

**Girls Under 21** (1940)
US 41 × 27 in. (104 × 69 cm)

Marketed as a cheap exploitation film, *Under Age* was in fact directed by the renowned **Edward Dmytryk** (1908–1999). Dmytryk started his film career in the early 20s as a messenger boy at Paramount. Over the next decade, he slowly climbed the corporate ladder and began directing in 1935. With 57 titles to his name, his most enduring works include the noir classics *Murder, My Sweet* (1944) and *Crossfire* (1947). Ultimately, however, Dmytryk is perhaps best known as being one of the legendary 'Hollywood Ten'. In 1947, the director was accused of being a member of the Communist Party. When questioned by the House Un-American Activities Committee, he refused to cooperate and was blacklisted by the government and sentenced to over a year in prison. In order to clear his name, he later renounced communism and testified against other Hollywood figures. In the 70s Dmytryk stopped directing altogether and spent the last twenty years of his life teaching film studies at university level and writing several books.

**Under Age** (1941)
US 41 × 27 in. (104 × 69 cm)
Courtesy of the Tony Nourmand Collection

**City Of Missing Girls** (1941)
US 41 × 27 in. (104 × 69 cm)
Courtesy of the Tony Nourmand Collection

Vice and prostitution films like *City Of Missing Girls* and *What Price Innocence?* provided exploitation producers with plenty of opportunity to show nudity and sex. But in doing so they had to pay due regard to the powers of censors and local police. They therefore often travelled with several versions of the same film. In a state with strict laws, or when trying to get a film passed by the Production Code Office, the producers would show a modest, innuendo-free, 'cold' version of their film, leaving the so-called 'hot' version to be wheeled out when the coast was clear. The roadshowers would also often carry a 'square-up reel' with them. This was about ten minutes long and was usually a filmed strip show or other nude footage. If the producer had been forced to show a 'cold' version of his film, he could wait until the local police were satisfied and had left the scene before projecting the forbidden full-frontal nudity that kept many a male audience happy.

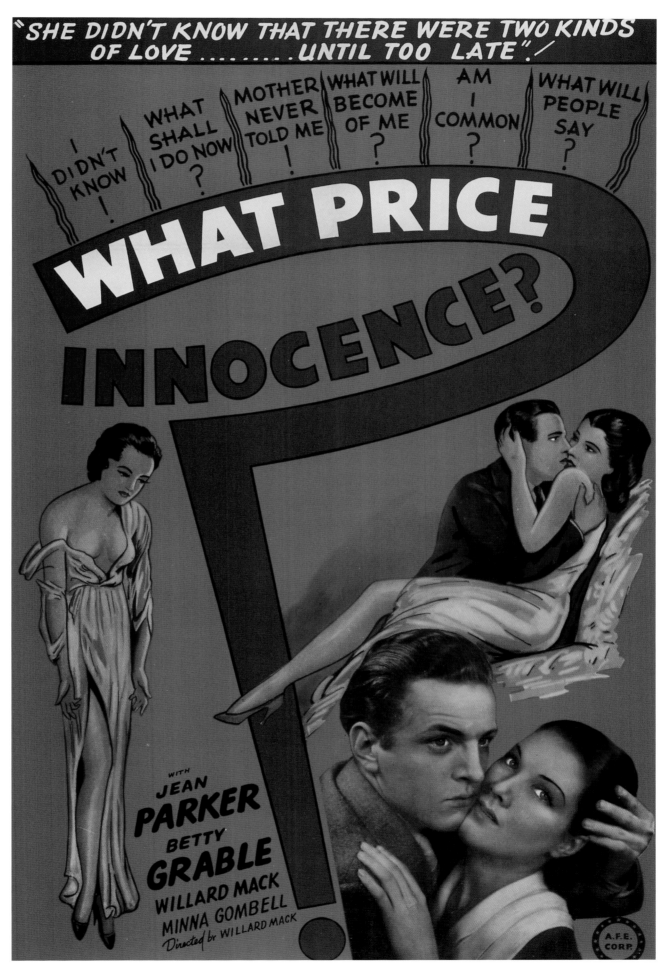

**What Price Innocence?** (1933)
US 41 × 27 in. (104 × 69 cm)
Courtesy of the Tony Nourmand Collection

**Hard, Fast And Beautiful** (1951)
US 36 × 14 in. (91 × 36 cm)
Courtesy of the Tony Nourmand Collection

*Young Man With A Horn* is a fairly tame love story from Warner Brothers yet the title and tagline were engineered to arouse maximum interest. A little too *risqué* for British censors, the tagline was discarded and the title changed to *Young Man Of Music* for the film's UK release.

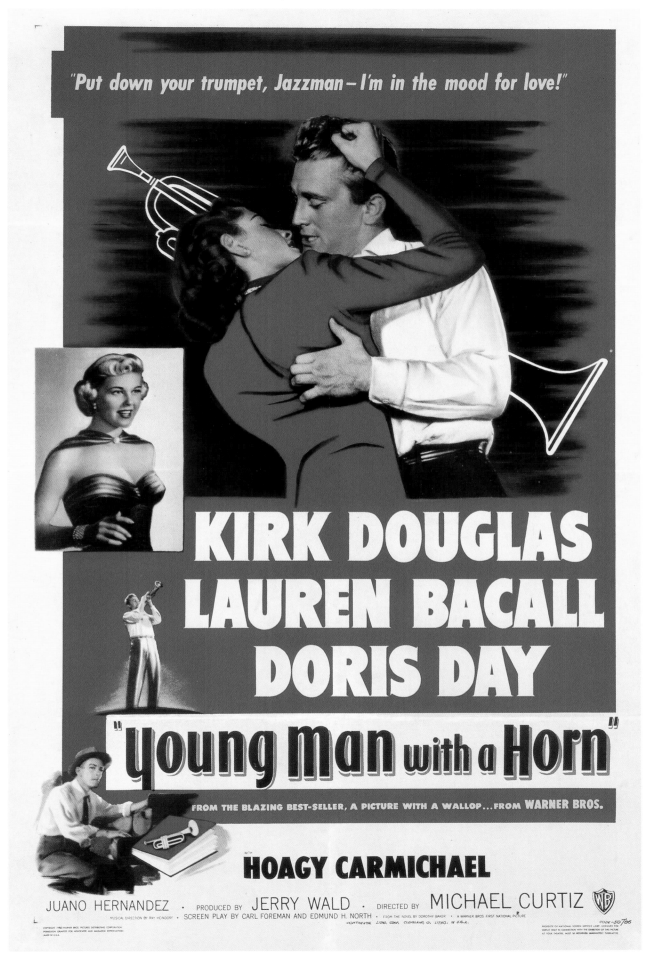

**Young Man With A Horn** (1950)
US 41 × 27 in. (104 × 69 cm)
Courtesy of the Tony Nourmand Collection

**Koroshi No Rakuin (Branded To Kill)** (1967)
Japanese 30 × 20 in. (76 × 51 cm)
Courtesy of the Tony Nourmand Collection

From the late 50s up until 1967, **Seijun Suzuki** (b. 1923) directed run-of-the-mill genre films for the Japanese Nikkatsu Studios. During this period he made some forty pictures and developed a reputation as a unique and disruptive voice in Japanese cinema. In the 60s, he used themes of ultra-violence that centred on the illicit activities of the Japanese mafia – the so-called *Yakuza*. (The word 'yakuza' literally denotes 8-9-3 in Japanese. Ya means 8, ku 9 and za 3. It comes from Japan's counterpart to Black Jack, Oicho-Kabu.) He also directed sado-masochistic soft-core sex films, called *'pinku eiga'*. Throughout his career at Nikkatsu, Suzuki adamantly asserted his uniqueness. Such individualism led to his *Tokyo Drifter* being censured by studio heads in 1966. But Suzuki stuck to his guns and made a final film with Nikkatsu the following year. *Branded To Kill* was a rococo, nihilistic and absurdly bizarre creation. It resulted in his dismissal from the studio and provoked widespread condemnation from the Japanese film industry. For the next ten years, Suzuki was forced to limit his filmmaking activities to television. But by the 80s, Japanese film studios were adopting a more liberal approach and the risks Suzuki had taken finally paid off. Once again able to make cinematic productions, Suzuki emerged as an internationally renowned director, picking up awards around the globe.

Another Japanese director whose films combine sex and violence is **Yasuharu Hasebe**. Recognized only in the world of Japanese 'B' movies, Hasebe specializes in subversive underground themes. His *Black Tight Killers* was picked up by exploitation producers in America who instantly saw the potential of a cheap foreign movie that would prove profitable in the drive-in market.

**Ore Ni Sawara To Abunaize (Black Tight Killers)** (1966)
US 41 × 27 in. (104 × 69 cm)
Courtesy of the Tony Nourmand Collection

**Switchblade Sisters** (1975)
US 41 × 27 in. (104 × 69 cm)
Art by J. Solie
Courtesy of the Tony Nourmand Collection

*Switchblade Sisters* and *Prison Girls* are 'girl-gang' movies that combine the typical 70s exploitation elements of sex and violence. The former is based very loosely on Shakespeare's *Othello* and, due to its camp humour and clever dialogue, has become a cult classic. It is one of Quentin Tarantino's favourite films and he sponsored its theatrical re-release in 1996.

*Prison Girls* enhanced its exploitable potential by adding 3D to the mix. Invented in 1838, stereoscopy was applied to create the illusion of a third dimension. Although used in film by the Lumière brothers as early as 1903, 3D really took off in the 50s with the success of United Artists' *Bwana Devil* (1952). Although expensive, 3D was a gimmick that could be put to use to capture audiences: a perfect device for otherwise average exploitation flicks like *Prison Girls*.

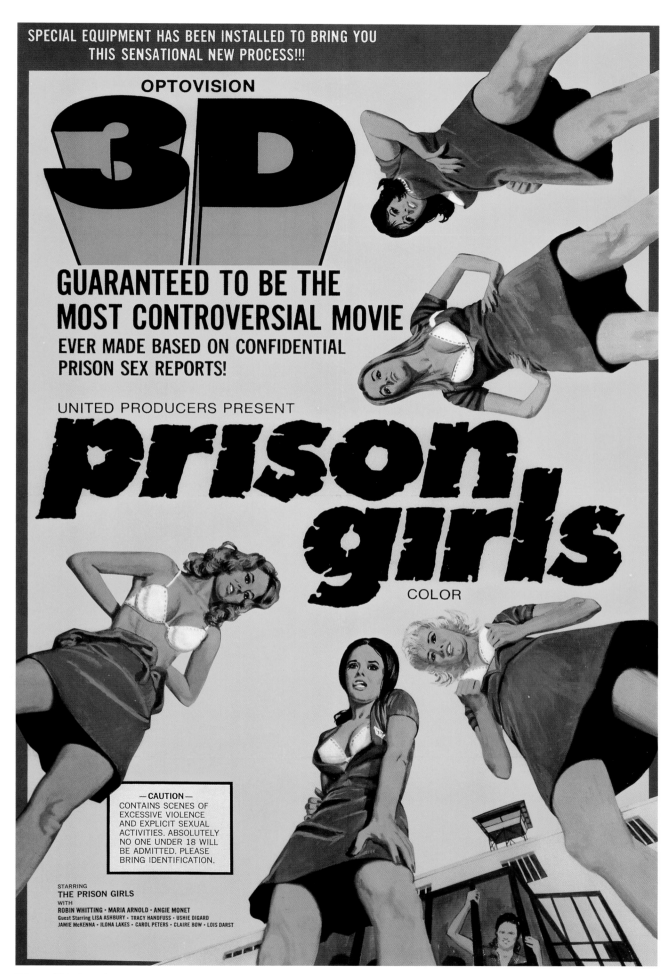

**Prison Girls** (1972)
US 41 × 27 in. (104 × 69 cm)
Courtesy of the Tony Nourmand Collection

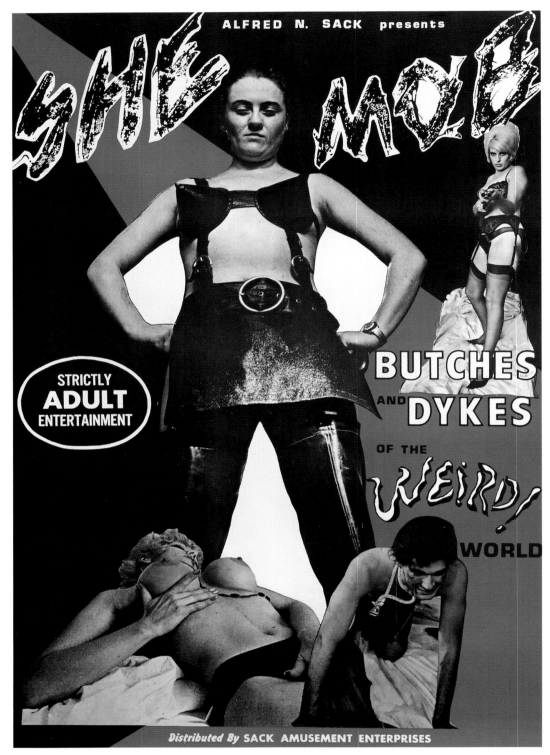

**She Mob** (1968)
US 41 × 27 in. (104 × 69 cm)
Courtesy of the Tony Nourmand Collection

It was the illustrious Martin Scorsese who was originally hired to direct *The Honeymoon Killers*. This would have been his first major project but, fatefully, Scorsese was replaced by **Leonard Kastle** (b. 1929). *The Honeymoon Killers* was Kastle's first foray into the world of directing and it was to be his last. He had initially intended the film to be called *Dear Martha*, but was overruled by producers who wanted a title with greater exploitability. Played to the music of Gustav Mahler, the film is clearly lurid and sensationalist but with a *Nouvelle Vague* feel. French New Wave director François Truffaut named it his favourite American film and it continues to have a strong following today.

*The Honeymoon Killers* was based on the true story of Martha Beck and Raymond Fernandez, two infamous serial killers in the 40s. Dubbed 'The Lonely Heart Killers' by the press, they were eventually caught and executed in Sing Sing prison in San Quentin in 1951.

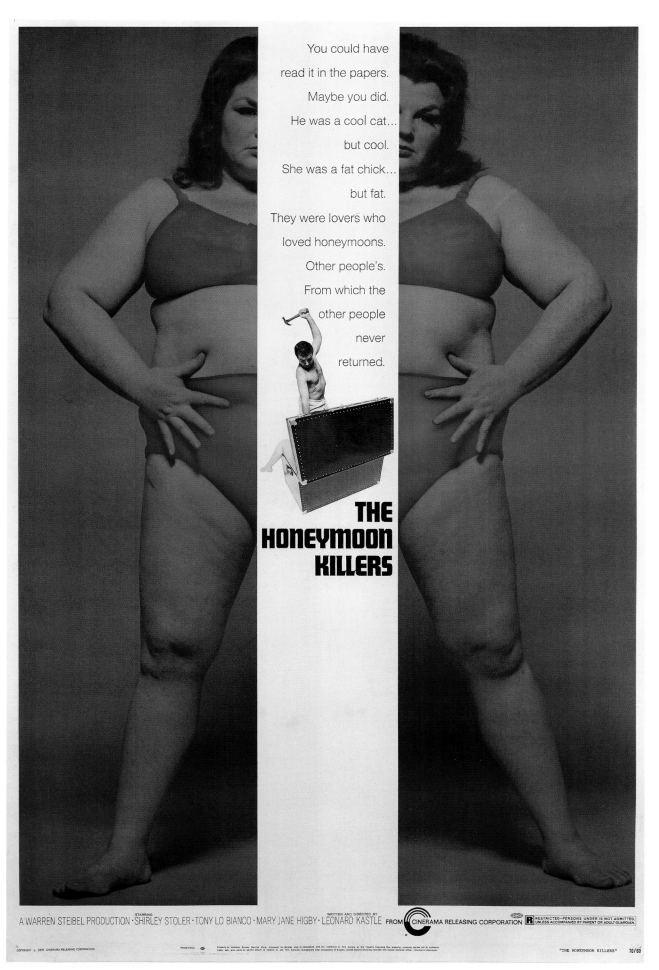

**The Honeymoon Killers** (1969)
US 60 × 40 in. (152 × 102 cm)
Courtesy of the Tony Nourmand Collection

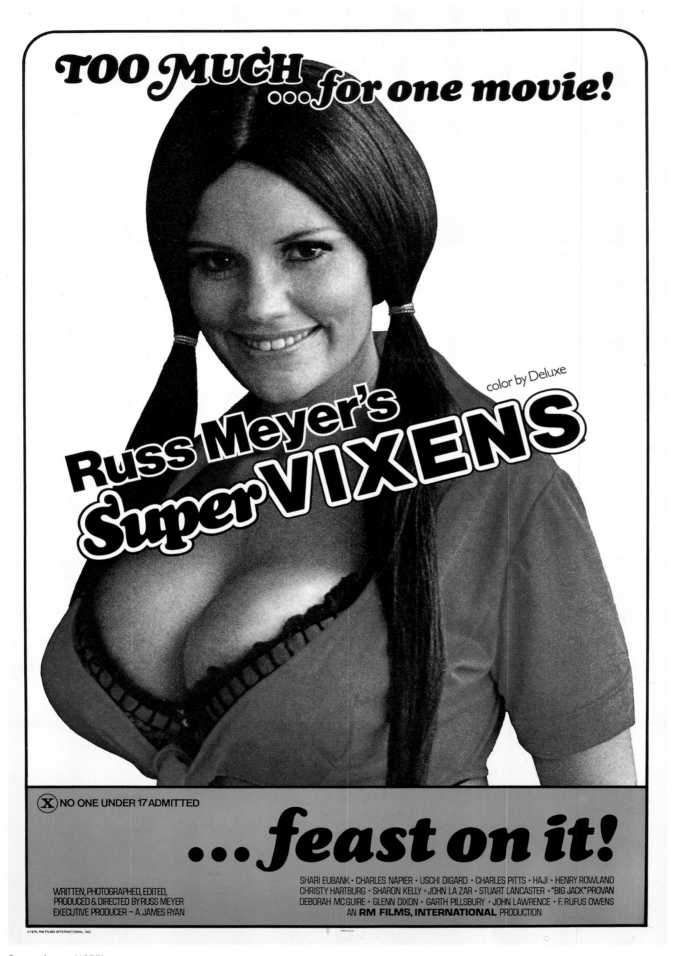

**Supervixens** (1975)
US 41 × 27 in. (104 × 69 cm)
Courtesy of the Tony Nourmand Collection

# TITLE INDEX

# ARTIST, DESIGNER AND PHOTOGRAPHER INDEX